SCIENTIFIC METHOD

Name _____

Put the following steps of the scientific method in the proper order.

_____ Research the problem.

_____ Observe and record.

_____ Make a hypothesis.

_____ Identify the problem.

_____ Arrive at a conclusion.

_____ Test the hypothesis.

Match the following terms with the correct definition.

_____ 1. hypothesis

_____ 2. control

_____ 3. variable

_____ 4. experiment

_____ 5. conclusion

_____ 6. theory

_____ 7. data

a) organized process used to test a hypothesis

b) an educated guess about the solution to a problem

c) observations and measurements recorded during an experiment

d) a judgment based on the results of an experiment

e) a logical explanation for events that occur in nature

f) used to show that the result of an experiment is really due to the condition being tested

g) factor that changes in an experiment

SAFETY IN THE LABORATORY

Name _____

What is wrong in the following pictures?

1.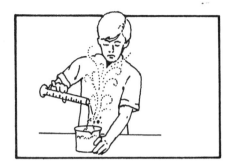

_____
_____
_____
_____

2.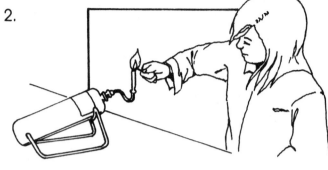

_____
_____
_____
_____

3.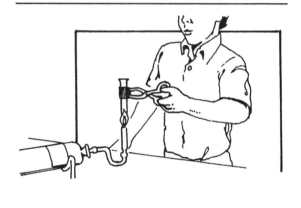

_____
_____
_____
_____

4.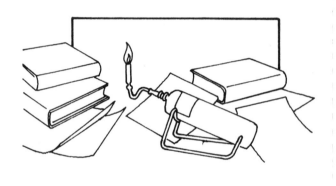

_____
_____
_____
_____

5.

_____
_____
_____
_____

6.

_____
_____
_____
_____

LABORATORY EQUIPMENT

Name _____

Match the following names of lab instruments and equipment with the correct picture.

a. beaker
b. graduated cylinder
c. balance
d. Bunsen burner
e. test tube
f. test tube clamp
g. funnel
h. Erlenmeyer flask
i. tongs
j. ring stand

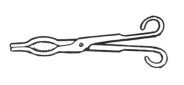

_____

_____

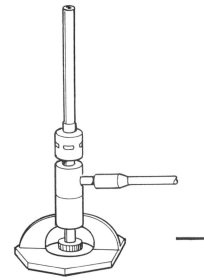

_____

_____

_____

_____

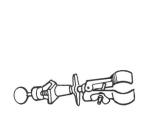

_____

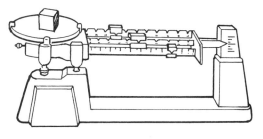

_____

USING THE BALANCE

The following balance measure mass is grams. What masses are shown on each of the following balances?

Answer: _____

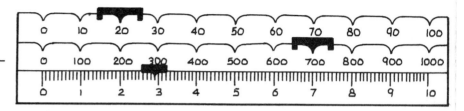

Answer: _____

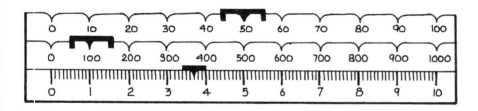

Answer: _____

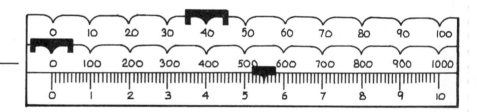

Answer: _____

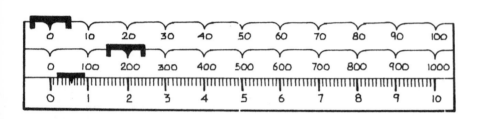

Answer: _____

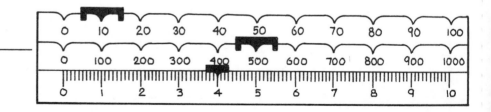

4

MEASURING LENGTH

What lengths are marked on the following centimeter ruler?

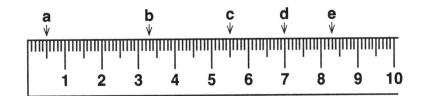

	cm	mm
a)	_____	_____
b)	_____	_____
c)	_____	_____
d)	_____	_____
e)	_____	_____

Measure the following lines with a centimeter ruler.

f) ▬▬▬▬▬▬▬▬   _____

g) ▬▬▬▬▬▬▬▬▬▬▬   _____

h) ▬▬▬▬▬▬▬▬▬▬▬▬▬▬▬▬▬▬▬   _____

i) ▬▬▬   _____

j) ▬▬▬▬▬▬▬▬▬▬▬▬▬▬   _____

k) ▬▬▬▬▬▬▬▬▬▬▬▬▬▬▬▬   _____

l) ▬   _____

MEASURING LIQUIDS

What volume is indicated on each of these graduated cylinders? The unit of volume of
is mL.

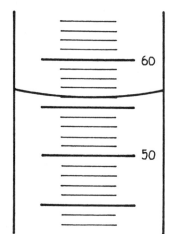

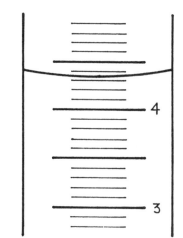

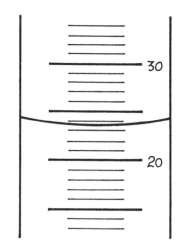

a) _____

b) _____

c) _____

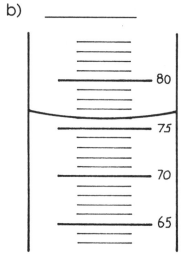

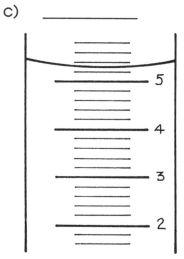

d) _____

e) _____

f) _____

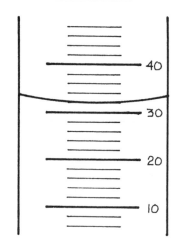

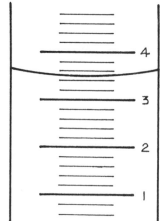

g) _____

h) _____

i) _____

6

READING THERMOMETERS

Name _____

What temperature is indicated on each of these thermometers?

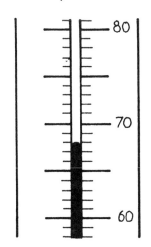

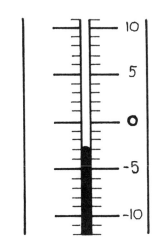

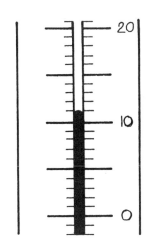

a) _____

b) _____

c) _____

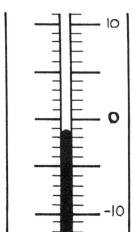

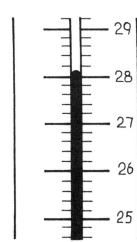

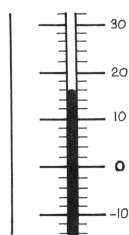

d) _____

e) _____

f) _____

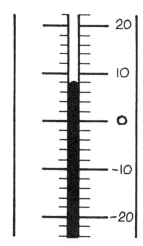

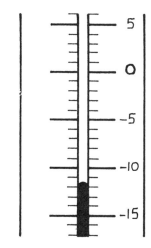

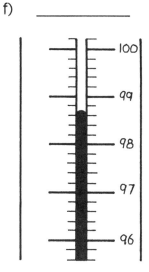

g) _____

h) _____

i) _____

METRICS AND MEASUREMENT

Name _____

Scientists use the metric system of measurement, based on the number 10. It is important to be able to convert from one unit to another.

kilo	hecto	deca	Basic Unit	deci	centi	milli
(k)	(h)	(da)	gram (g)	(d)	(c)	(m)
1000	100	10	liter (L)	.1	.01	.001
10^3	10^2	10^1	meter (m)	10^{-1}	10^{-2}	10^{-3}

Using the above chart, we can determine how many places to move the decimal point and in what direction by counting the places from one unit to the other.

Example: Convert 5 mL to L.

Answer: To go from milli (m) to the basic unit, liters, count on the above chart three places to the left. Move the decimal point three places to the left and 5 mL becomes 0.005 L.

Convert the following.

1. 35 mL = _____ dL

2. 950 g = _____ kg

3. 275 mm = _____ cm

4. 1,000 L = _____ kL

5. 1,000 mL = _____ L

6. 4,500 mg = _____ g

7. 25 cm = _____ mm

8. 0.005 kg = _____ dag

9. 0.075 m = _____ cm

10. 15 g = _____ mg

UNIT CONVERSIONS AND FACTOR-LABEL METHOD

Name _____

Another method of going from one unit to another involves multiplying by a conversion factor. A conversion factor is a fraction that is equal to the number 1. For example, 60 seconds = 1 hour. Therefore, 60 sec/1 hr or 1 hr/60 sec = 1. When you multiply by the number 1, the value of the number is not changed, although the units may be different.

Example: How many milligrams in 20 kilograms?

Solution: Use the following relationships:

$$1000 \text{ mg} = 1 \text{ g}$$
$$1000 \text{ g} = 1 \text{ kg}$$

1. Start with the original number and unit.
2. Multiply by a unit factor with the unit to be discarded on the bottom and the desired unit on top.
3. Cancel units.
4. Perform numerical calculations.

$$20 \text{ kg} \times \frac{1000 \text{ g}}{1 \text{ kg}} \times \frac{1000 \text{ mg}}{1 \text{ g}} = 20,000,000 \text{ or } 2 \times 10^7 \text{ mg}$$

Perform the following conversions using unit factoring.

1. 500 mL = _____ L

2. 25 cg = _____ g

3. 400 mg = _____ kg

4. 30 cm = _____ mm

5. 3500 secs = _____ hr

6. 2 yrs = _____ secs (Assume 1 year = 365 days)

7. 15 m = _____ mm

8. 0.75 L = _____ mL

9. 6.4 kg = _____ g

10. 7200 m = _____ km

11. 4.2 L = _____ cm^3

12. 0.35 km = _____ m

13. 2.3 L = _____ mL

14. 4.5 yds = _____ in

15. 50 mm = _____ km

16. 150 mg = _____ g

17. 150 kg = _____ g

18. 23 mL = _____ L

19. 0.156 g = _____ mg

20. 1.25 L = _____ mL

USING CORRECT UNITS

Name _____

For each of the following commonly used measurements, indicate its symbol. Use the symbols to complete the following.

_____ milliliter   _____ milligram   _____ liter   _____ centimeter

_____ kilogram   _____ millimeter   _____ kilometer   _____ gram

_____ meter   _____ millisecond   _____ microgram   _____ nanometer

1. Colas may be purchased in two or three _____ bottles.

2. The mass of bowling ball is 7.25 _____ .

3. The length of the common housefly is about 1 _____ .

4. The mass of a paper clip is about 1 _____ .

5. One teaspoon of cough syrup has a volume of 5 _____ .

6. The speed limit on the highway is usually 106.6 _____ /h or 29 _____ /s.

7. The length of the small intestine in man is about 6.25 _____ .

8. Viruses such as AIDS, polio and flu range in length from 17 to 1000 _____ .

9. Adults require 1,000 _____ of calcium to meet the U.S. RDA.

10. In a vacuum, light can travel 300 km in 1 _____ .

11. The mass of a proton is 1.67×10^{-18} _____ .

12. Blue light has a wavelength of about 500 _____ .

13. One mole of oxygen gas at STP occupies 22.4 _____ .

14. Myoglobin, a protein that stores oxygen, has a mass of 2.98×10^{-14} _____ .

15. Buttery popcorn contained in a large 1 _____ bowl has a mass of about 50 _____ of fat and about 650 calories.

16. The dying comet fragments that continued to batter Jupiter travel at speeds of about 58,117 _____ / _____ or 130,000 miles per hour.

17. The human heart has a mass of about 1.05 _____ .

18. Stand with your arms raised out to your side. The distance from your nose to your outstretched middle finger is about 1 _____ .

19. The body mass of a flea is about 0.5 _____ and it can jump about 20 _____ high.

20. On a statistical basis, smoking a single cigarette lowers your life expectancy by 642,000 _____ or 10.7 minutes.

SCIENTIFIC NOTATION

Name _____

Scientists very often deal with very small and very large numbers, which can lead to a lot of confusion when counting zeros! We have learned to express these numbers as powers of 10.

Scientific notation takes the form of M x 10^n where $1 \leq M < 10$ and n represents the number of decimal places to be moved. Positive n indicates the standard form is larger than zero, whereas negative n would indicate a number smaller than zero.

Example 1: Convert 1,500,000 to scientific notation.

Move the decimal point so that there is only one digit to its left, a total of 6 places.

$1,500,000 = 1.5 \times 10^6$

Example 2: Convert 0.00025 to scientific notation.

For this, move the decimal point 4 places to the right.

$0.00025 = 2.5 \times 10^{-4}$

(Note that when a number starts out less than one, the exponent is always negative.)

Convert the following to scientific notation.

1. 0.005 = _____

2. 5,050 = _____

3. 0.0008 = _____

4. 1,000 = _____

5. 1,000,000 = _____

6. 0.25 = _____

7. 0.025 = _____

8. 0.0025 = _____

9. 500 = _____

10. 5,000 = _____

Convert the following to standard notation.

1. 1.5×10^3 = _____

2. 1.5×10^{-3} = _____

3. 3.75×10^{-2} = _____

4. 3.75×10^2 = _____

5. 2.2×10^5 = _____

6. 3.35×10^{-1} = _____

7. 1.2×10^{-4} = _____

8. 1×10^4 = _____

9. 1×10^{-1} = _____

10. 4×10^0 = _____

CALCULATIONS USING SIGNIFICANT FIGURES

Name _____

When multiplying numbers in scientific notation, multiply the first part of the number (mantissa) and add exponents.

Example 1: $(3.0 \times 10^2)(2.5 \times 10^6) =$

Answer: Multiply $3.0 \times 2.5 = 7.5$
Add $2 + 6 = 8$
$= 7.5 \times 10^8$

When dividing numbers in scientific notation, divide the first part of the number and subtract exponents.

Example 2: $\dfrac{9.0 \times 10^6}{4.5 \times 10^2}$

Answer: Divide 9.0 by $4.5 = 2.0$
Subtract 2 from $6 = 4$
$= 2.0 \times 10^4$

Perform the following calculations. Express all answers in scientific notation.

1. $(1.5 \times 10^3)(3.5 \times 10^5)$	6. $(4 \times 10^5) \div (1 \times 10^{-3})$
2. $(2.0 \times 10^8)(2.0 \times 10^6)$	7. $(7.6 \times 10^{-3})(8.2 \times 10^{-4})$
3. $(6.2 \times 10^6) \div (3.1 \times 10^2)$	8. $(8.5 \times 10^{-8}) \div (2.5 \times 10^{-3})$
4. $(5.0 \times 10^4) \div (2.5 \times 10^3)$	9. $(7.0 \times 10^{11})(7.0 \times 10^{-11})$
5. $(6.8 \times 10^7)(2.2 \times 10^{-5})$	10. $(1.3 \times 10^{-5}) \div (2.6 \times 10^{-9})$

DENSITY

Name _____

Which has the greater mass, air or lead? Most of you would answer lead, but actually this question does not have an answer. To compare these two things you need to now how much of each you have. A large amount of air could have a greater mass than a small amount of lead. To compare different things, we have to compare the masses of each that occupy the same space, or volume. This is called density.

$$\text{density} = \frac{\text{mass}}{\text{volume}}$$

Solve the following problems.

1. What is the density of carbon dioxide gas if 0.196 g occupies a volume of 100 mL?

   Answer: _____

2. A block of wood 3.0 cm on each side has a mass of 27 g. What is the density of this block?

   Answer: _____

3. An irregularly shaped stone was lowered into a graduated cylinder holding a volume of water equal to 2.0 mL. The height of the water rose to 7.0 mL. If the mass of the stone was 25 g, what was its density?

   Answer: _____

4. A 10.0 cm³ sample of copper has a mass of 89.6 g. What is the density of copper?

   Answer: _____

5. Silver has a density of 10.5 g/cm³ and gold has a density of 19.3 g/cm³. Which would have a greater mass, 5 cm³ of silver or 5 cm³ of gold?

   Answer: _____

6. Five mL of ethanol has a mass of 3.9 g, and 5.0 mL of benzene has a mass of 4.4 g. Which liquid is denser?

   Answer: _____

7. A sample of iron has the dimensions of 2 cm x 3 cm x 2 cm. If the mass of this rectangular-shaped object is 94 g, what is the density of iron?

   Answer: _____

GRAPHING OF DATA

Name _____

Graphing is a very important tool in science since it enables us to see trends that are not always obvious. Graph the following data and answer the questions below.

Mass of Liquid (g)	Volume of Liquid (cm³)
20	4
100	20
75	15
40	8
10	2

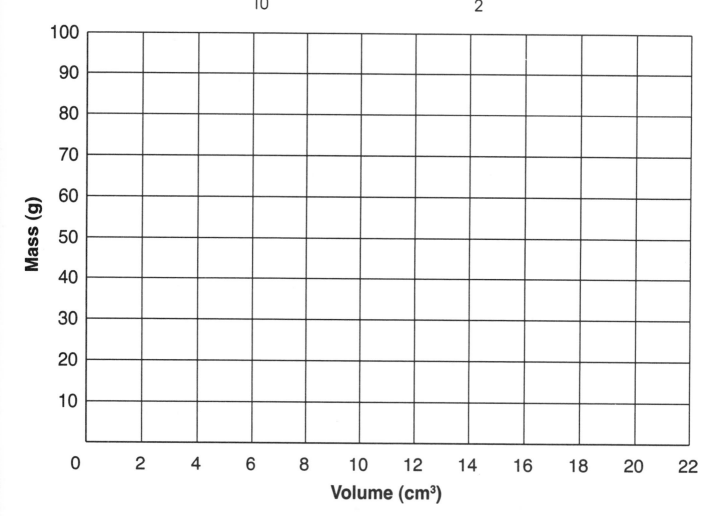

1. As mass increases, what happens to the volume? _____

2. As volume increases, what happens to the mass? _____

3. How many grams would occupy 12 mL? _____

4. What volume would 90 g occupy? _____

5. What is the density of the liquid? _____

DETERMINING SPEED (VELOCITY)

Name _____

Speed is a measure of how fast an object is moving or traveling. Velocity is a measure of how fast an object is traveling in a certain direction. Both speed and velocity include the distance traveled compared to the amount of time taken to cover this distance.

$$\text{speed} = \frac{\text{distance}}{\text{time}} \qquad \text{velocity} = \frac{\text{distance}}{\text{time}} \quad \text{in a specific direction}$$

Answer the following questions.

1. What is the velocity of a car that traveled a total of 75 kilometers north in 1.5 hours?
   _____

2. What is the velocity of a plane that traveled 3,000 miles from New York to California in 5.0 hours? _____

3. John took 45 minutes to bicycle to his grandmother's house, a total of four kilometers. What was his velocity in km/hr? _____

4. It took 3.5 hours for a train to travel the distance between two cities at a velocity of 120 miles/hr. How many miles lie between the two cities? _____

5. How long would it take for a car to travel a distance of 200 kilometers if it is traveling at a velocity of 55 km/hr? _____

6. A car is traveling at 100 km/hr. How many hours will it take to cover a distance of 750 km? _____

7. A plane traveled for about 2.5 hours at a velocity of 1200 km/hr. What distance did it travel? _____

8. A girl is pedaling her bicycle at a velocity of 0.10 km/min. How far will she travel in two hours? _____

9. An ant carries food at a speed of 1 cm/s. How long will it take the ant to carry a cookie crumb from the kitchen table to the ant hill, a distance of 50 m? Express your answer in seconds, minutes and hours. _____

10. The water in the Buffalo River flows at an average speed of 5 km/hr. If you and a friend decide to canoe down the river a distance of 16 kilometers, how many hours and minutes will it take? _____

CALCULATING AVERAGE SPEED

Name _____

Graph the following data on the grid below and answer the questions at the bottom of the page.

Time (min)	Distance (m)
0	0
1	50
2	75
3	90
4	110
5	125

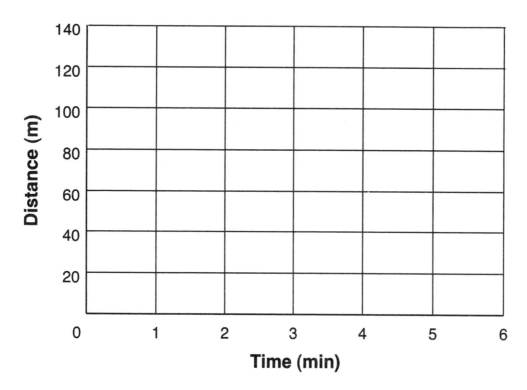

Average Speed = $\dfrac{\text{Total Distance}}{\text{Total Time}}$

1. What is the average speed after two minutes? _____

2. After three minutes? _____

3. After five minutes? _____

4. What is the average speed between two and four minutes? _____

5. What is the average speed between four and five minutes? _____

ACCELERATION CALCULATIONS

Name _____

Acceleration means a change in speed or direction. It can also be defined as a change in velocity per unit of time.

$$a = \frac{v_f - v_i}{t}$$ where a = velocity
v_f = final velocity
v_i = initial velocity
t = time

Calculate the acceleration for the following data.

	Initial Velocity	Final Velocity	Time	Acceleration
1.	0 km/hr	24 km/hr	3 s	_____
2.	0 m/s	35 m/s	5 s	_____
3.	20 km/hr	60 km/hr	10 s	_____
4.	50 m/s	150 m/s	5 s	_____
5.	25 km/hr	1200 km/hr	2 min	_____

6. A car accelerates from a standstill to 60 km/hr in 10.0 seconds.
   What is its acceleration?   _____

7. A car accelerates from 25 km/hr to 55 km/hr in 30 seconds.
   What is its acceleration?   _____

8. A train is accelerating at a rate of 2.0 km/hr/s.
   If its initial velocity is 20 km/hr, what is its velocity after 30 seconds?   _____

9. A runner achieves a velocity of 11.1 m/s 9 s after he begins.
   What is his acceleration?   _____
   What distance did he cover?   _____

GRAPHING SPEED VS. TIME

Name _____

Plot the following data on the graph and answer the questions below.

Speed (km/hr)	Time (s)
0.0	0
10.0	2
20.0	4
30.0	6
40.0	8
50.0	10

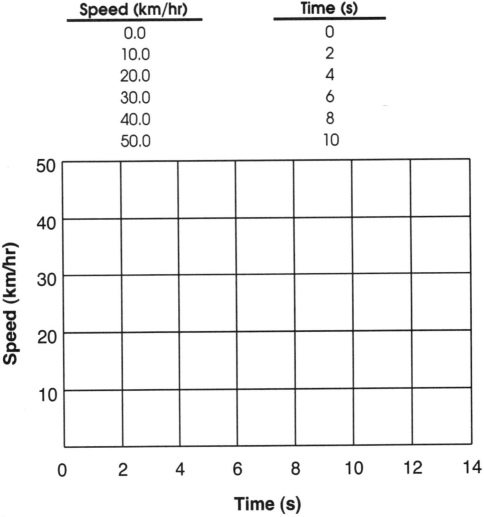

1. As time increases, what happens to the speed? _____

2. What is the speed at 5 s? _____

3. Assuming constant acceleration, what would be the speed at 14 s?

   _____

4. At what time would the object reach a speed of 45 km/hr? _____

5. What is the object's acceleration? _____

6. What would the shape of the graph be if a speed of 50.0 km/hr is maintained from
   10 s to 20 s? _____

7. Based on the information in Problem 6, calculate the acceleration from 10 s to 20 s.

   _____

8. What would the shape of the graph be if the speed of the object decreased from
   50.0 km/hr at 20 s to 30 km/hr at 40 s? _____

9. What is the acceleration in Problem 8? _____

GRAPHING DISTANCE VS. TIME

Name _____

Plot the following data on the graph and answer the questions below.

Distance (km)	Time (s)
0	0
5	10
12	20
20	30
30	40
42	50
56	60

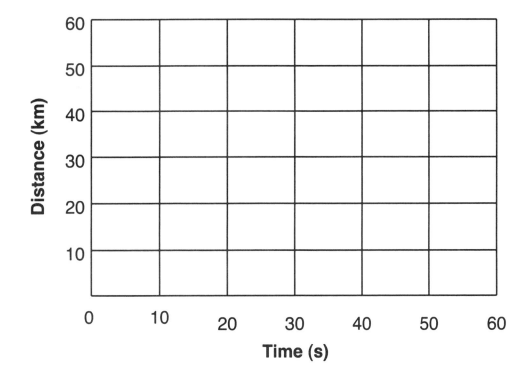

1. What is the average speed at t = 20 s? _____

2. What is the average speed at t = 30 s? _____

3. What is the acceleration between 20 s and 30 s? _____

4. What is the average speed at t = 40 s? _____

5. What is the average speed at t = 60 s? _____

6. What is the acceleration between 40 s and 60 s? _____

7. Is the object accelerating at a constant rate? _____

GRAVITY AND ACCELERATION (I)

Name _____

The acceleration of a freely falling body is 9.8 m/sec/sec due to the force of gravity.

Using the formula, $a = \dfrac{v_f - v_i}{t}$, we can calculate the velocity of a falling object

at any time if the initial velocity is known.

Example: What is the velocity of a rubber ball dropped from a building roof after 5 seconds?

Answer: $9.8 \text{ m/sec/sec} = \dfrac{v_f - 0}{5 \text{ sec}}$

$v_f = 49 \text{ m/sec}$

Solve the following problems.

1. What is the velocity of a quarter dropped from a tower after 10 seconds?

   Answer: _____

2. If a block of wood dropped from a tall building has attained a velocity of 78.4 m/s, how long has it been falling?

   Answer: _____

3. If a ball that is freely falling has attained a velocity of 19.6 m/s after two seconds, what is its velocity five seconds later?

   Answer: _____

4. A piece of metal has attained a velocity of 107.8 m/sec after falling for 10 seconds. What is its initial velocity?

   Answer: _____

5. How long will it take an object that falls from rest to attain a velocity of 147 m/sec?

   Answer: _____

GRAVITY AND ACCELERATION (II)

Name _____

The distance covered by a freely falling body is calculated by the following formula,

$$d = \frac{at^2}{2}$$

where d = distance
       a = acceleration
       t = time

Example 1: How far will an object fall in 5 seconds?

Answer: $d = \frac{9.8 \text{ m/s}^2)\ (5s)^2}{2} = 122.5$ meters

Example 2: What is the average velocity of a ball that attains a velocity of 39.2 m/s after 4 seconds?

Answer: $v_a = \frac{v_f - v_i}{2} = \frac{39.2 - 0}{2} = 19.6$ m/s

Solve the following problems.

1. How far will a rubber ball fall in 10 seconds?

   Answer: _____

2. How far will a rubber ball fall in 20 seconds?

   Answer: _____

3. How long will it take an object dropped from a window to fall a distance of 78.4 meters?

   Answer: _____

4. Calculate the final velocity of the ball in Problem 1.

   Answer: _____

5. What is the average velocity of the ball in Problem 1?

   Answer: _____

6. An airplane is traveling at an altitude of 31,360 meters. A box of supplies is dropped from its cargo hold. How long will it take to reach the ground?

   Answer: _____

7. At what velocity will the box in Problem 6 be traveling when it hits the ground?

   Answer: _____

8. What is the average velocity of the box in Problem 6?

   Answer: _____

FORCE DIAGRAMS

Name _____

Find the resultant force in each of the following diagrams and draw the resultant vector. Use a ruler and a protractor where necessary. Scale: 1 cm = 10 N, where N represents newtons of force.

1.

20 N   30 N

2.

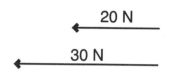

20 N

30 N

3.

30 N

30 N

4.

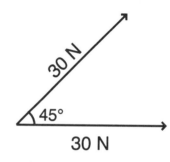

30 N

45°

30 N

5.

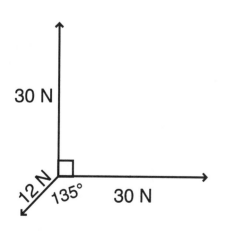

30 N

12 N   135°   30 N

6.

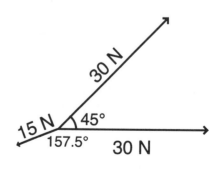

30 N

15 N   45°

157.5°   30 N

FORCE AND ACCELERATION

Name _____

A force is a push or a pull. To calculate force, we use the following formula,

$$F = ma$$ where   F = force in newtons
m = mass in kg
a = acceleration in m/sec^2

Example: With what force will a rubber ball hit the ground if it has a mass of 0.25 kg?

Answer: F = (0.25 kg) (9.8 m/s^2)
F = 2.45 N

Solve the following problems.

1. With what force will a car hit a tree if the car has a mass of 3,000 kg and it is accelerating at a rate of 2 m/s^2?

    Answer: _____

2. A 10 kg bowling ball would require what force to accelerate it down an alleyway at a rate of 3 m/s^2?

    Answer: _____

3. What is the mass of a falling rock if it hits the ground with a force of 147 newtons?

    Answer: _____

4. What is the acceleration of a softball if it has a mass of 0.50 kg and hits the catcher's glove with a force of 25 newtons?

    Answer: _____

5. What is the mass of a truck if it is accelerating at a rate of 5 m/s^2 and hits a parked car with a force of 14,000 newtons?

    Answer: _____

MOTION MATCHING

Name _____

Match the correct term in Column I with its definition in Column II.

I

1. _____ kinetic

2. _____ centripetal

3. _____ mass

4. _____ acceleration

5. _____ velocity

6. _____ weight

7. _____ gravity

8. _____ inertia

9. _____ speed

10. _____ momentum

11. _____ newton

II

a) amount of matter in an object

b) amount of force exerted on an object due to gravity

c) distance covered per unit of time

d) rate at which velocity changes over time

e) speed in a given direction

f) unit of measurement for force

g) energy of motion

h) tendency of a moving object to keep moving

i) depends on the mass and velocity of an object

j) type of force that keeps objects moving in a circle

k) attractive force between two objects

HEAT CALCULATIONS

Name _____

Heat is measured in units of joules or calories. The amount of heat given off or absorbed can be calculated by the following formula.

> $\Delta Q = m \times \Delta T \times C$
>
> heat = (mass in grams) (temperature change) (specific heat)
>
> The specific heat of water = 1.0 cal/g C° or 4.2 joules/g C°

Solve the following problems.

1. How many calories are absorbed by a pot of water with a mass of 500 g in order to raise the temperature from 20° C to 30° C?

   Answer: _____

2. How many joules would be absorbed for the water in Problem 1?

   Answer: _____

3. If the specific heat of iron = 0.46 J/g C°, how much heat is needed to warm 50 g of iron from 20° C to 100° C?

   Answer: _____

4. If it takes 105 calories to warm 100 g of aluminum from 20° C to 25° C, what is the specific heat of aluminum?

   Answer: _____

5. If it takes 31,500 joules of heat to warm 750 g of water, what was the temperature change?

   Answer: _____

HEAT AND PHASE CHANGES

Name _____

During a phase change, the temperature remains the same. For these calculations, we use the following formulas.

For freezing and melting, heat = (mass in grams) (heat of fusion)
For boiling and condensation, heat = (mass in grams) (heat of vaporization)
The heat of fusion of water = 340 J/g
The heat of vaporization of water = 2,300 J/g

Solve the following problems.

1. How many joules of heat are necessary to melt 500 g of ice at its freezing point?

   Answer: _____

2. How many kilojoules is this?

   Answer: _____

3. How much heat is necessary to vaporize 500 g of water at its boiling point?

   Answer: _____

4. If 5,100 joules of heat are given off when a sample of water freezes, what is the mass of the water?

   Answer: _____

5. If 57,500 joules of heat are given off when a sample of steam condenses, what is the mass of the steam?

   Answer: _____

SIMPLE MACHINES

Name _____

What types of simple machines are shown in the following pictures?

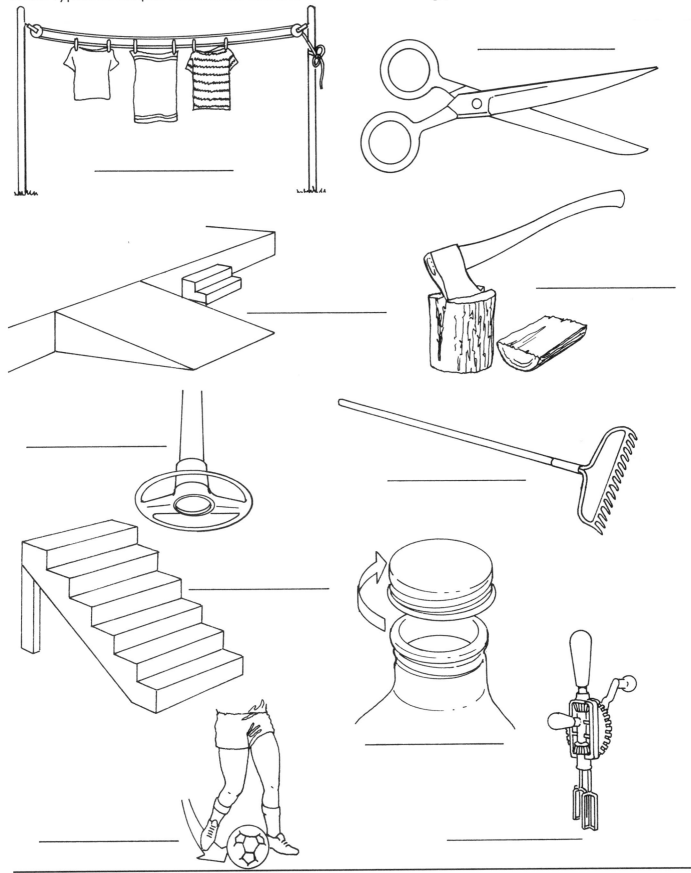

TYPES OF LEVERS

Classify the following levers as first, second or third class.

 _____

 _____

_____

_____

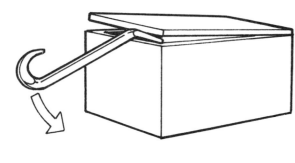

_____

 _____

 _____

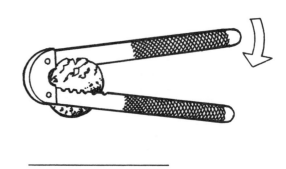

_____

POTENTIAL AND KINETIC ENERGY

Name _____

Potential energy is stored energy due to position. Kinetic energy is energy that depends on mass and velocity (movement).

Potential Energy = Weight x Height (P.E. = w x h)

Kinetic Energy = $\frac{1}{2}$ Mass x Velocity^2 (K.E. = $\frac{1}{2}mv^2$)

The units used are: Energy = joules
Weight = newtons
Height = meters
Mass = kilograms
Velocity = m/s

For a closed system, the sum of the potential energy and the kinetic energy is a constant. As the potential energy decreases, the kinetic energy increases.

Solve the following problems.

1. What is the potential energy of a rock that weighs 100 newtons that is sitting on top of a hill 300 meters high?

    Answer: _____

2. What is the kinetic energy of a bicycle with a mass of 14 kg traveling at a velocity of 3 m/s?

    Answer: _____

3. A flower pot weighing 3 newtons is sitting on a windowsill 30 meters from the ground. Is the energy of the flower pot potential or kinetic? How many joules is this?

    Answers: _____ _____

4. When the flower pot in Problem 3 is only 10 meters from the ground, what is its potential energy?

    Answer: _____

5. How much of the total energy in Problems 3 and 4 has been transformed to kinetic energy?

    Answer: _____

6. A 1200 kg automobile is traveling at a velocity of 100 m/s. Is its energy potential or kinetic? How much energy does it possess?

    Answers: _____ _____

CALCULATING WORK

Name _____

Work has a special meaning in science. It is the product of the force applied to an object and the distance the object moves. The unit of work is the joule (J).

> W = Force x Distance
> W = F x d
>
> Force = newtons
> Distance = meters

Solve the following problems.

1. A book weighing 1.0 newton is lifted 2 meters. How much work was done?

   Answer: _____

2. A force of 15 newtons is used to push a box along the floor a distance of 3 meters. How much work was done?

   Answer: _____

3. It took 50 joules to push a chair 5 meters across the floor. With what force was the chair pushed?

   Answer: _____

4. A force of 100 newtons was necessary to lift a rock. A total of 150 joules of work was done. How far was the rock lifted?

   Answer: _____

5. It took 500 newtons of force to push a car 4 meters. How much work was done?

   Answer: _____

6. A young man exerted a force of 9,000 newtons on a stalled car but was unable to move it. How much work was done?

   Answer: _____

MECHANICAL ADVANTAGE

Name _____

What is the mechanical advantage of the following simple machines?

$$MA = \frac{F_R}{F_E}$$ where F_R = resistance force
F_E = effort force

1.

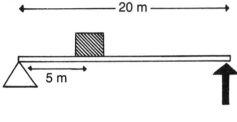

_____

2.

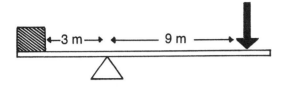

_____

3.

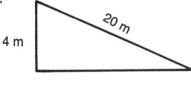

_____

4.

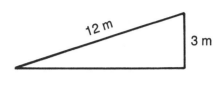

_____

5.

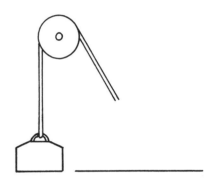

_____

6.

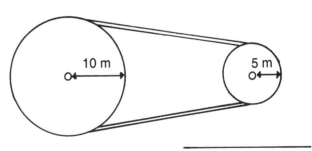

_____

7.

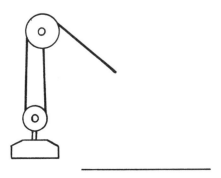

_____

8.

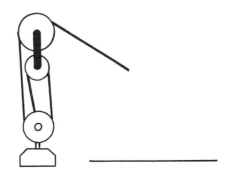

_____

CALCULATING EFFICIENCY

Name _____

The amount of work obtained from a machine is always less than the amount of work put into it. This is because some of the work is lost due to friction. The efficiency of a machine can be calculated using the following formula.

$$\text{percent efficiency} = \frac{\text{work output}}{\text{work input}} \times 100$$

What is the efficiency of the following machines?

1. A man expends 100 J of work to move a box up an inclined plane. The amount of work produced is 80 J.

   Answer: _____

2. A box weighing 100 newtons is pushed up an inclined plane that is 5 meters long. It takes a force of 75 newtons to push it to the top, which has a height of 3 meters.

   Answer: _____

3. Using a lever, a person applies 60 newtons of force and moves the lever 1 meter. This moves a 200 newton rock at the other end by 0.2 meters.

   Answer: _____

4. A person in a wheelchair exerts a force of 25 newtons to go up a ramp that is 10 meters long. The weight of the person and wheelchair is 60 newtons and the height of the ramp is 3 meters.

   Answer: _____

5. A boy pushes a lever down 2 meters with a force of 75 newtons. The box at the other end with a weight of 50 newtons moves up 2.5 meters.

   Answer: _____

6. A pulley system operates with 40% efficiency. If the work put in is 200 joules, how much useful work is produced?

   Answer: _____

CALCULATING POWER

Name _____

Power is the amount of work done per unit of time. The unit for power, joules/second, is the watt.

> Power = $\dfrac{\text{work}}{\text{time}}$
>
> work = joules
> time = seconds

Solve the following problems.

1. A set of pulleys is used to lift a piano weighing 1,000 newtons. The piano is lifted 3 meters in 60 seconds. How much power is used?

   Answer: _____

2. How much power is used if a force of 35 newtons is used to push a box a distance of 10 meters in 5 seconds?

   Answer: _____

3. What is the power of a kitchen blender if it can perform 3,750 joules of work in 15 seconds?

   Answer: _____

4. How much work is done using a 500-watt microwave oven for 5 minutes?

   Answer: _____

5. How much work is done using a 60-watt light bulb for 1 hour?

   Answer: _____

FORCE AND WORK CROSSWORD

Name _____

Across

3. Force times distance

4. Point around which a lever rotates

5. Amount of work done per unit of time

6. Can be considered a type of inclined plane wrapped around a cylinder

7. A machine makes work easier by reducing force and increasing _____ .

9. How many times a force is multiplied by a machine is the mechanical _____ .

11. An inclined plane is an example of a _____ machine.

Down

1. Unit of force

2. Unit for work (newton-meter)

4. Force that reduces the efficiency of a machine

8. Joule per second

10. Work output divided by work input.

12. An automobile is an example of a _____ machine.

SUBSTANCES VS. MIXTURES

A substance is matter for which a chemical formula can be written. Elements and compounds are substances. Mixtures can be in any proportion, and the parts are not chemically bonded.

Classify the following as to whether it is a substance or a mixture by writing S or M in the space provided.

1. sodium _____

2. water _____

3. soil _____

4. coffee _____

5. oxygen _____

6. alcohol _____

7. carbon dioxide _____

8. cake batter _____

9. air _____

10. soup _____

11. iron _____

12. salt water _____

13. ice cream _____

14. nitrogen _____

15. eggs _____

16. blood _____

17. table salt _____

18. nail polish _____

19. milk _____

20. cola _____

HOMOGENEOUS VS. HETEROGENEOUS MATTER

Name _____

Classify the following substances and mixtures as either homogeneous or heterogeneous. Place a √ in the correct column.

	HOMOGENEOUS	HETEROGENEOUS
1. flat soda pop		
2. cherry vanilla ice cream		
3. salad dressing		
4. sugar		
5. soil		
6. aluminum foil		
7. black coffee		
8. sugar water		
9. city air		
10. paint		
11. alcohol		
12. iron		
13. beach sand		
14. pure air		
15. spaghetti sauce		

SOLUTIONS, COLLOIDS AND SUSPENSIONS

Name _____

Label the following mixtures as a solution, colloid or suspension. Give an example of each.

1. large particles,

   settles out on standing

   Kind of mixture: _____

   Example: _____

2. medium size particles,

   settles out on standing

   scatters light

   Kind of mixture: _____

   Example: _____

3. very small particles

   does not settle out on standing

   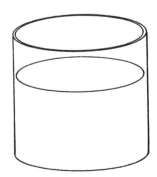

   Kind of mixture: _____

   Example: _____

PHYSICAL VS. CHEMICAL PROPERTIES

Name _____

A physical property is observed with the senses and can be determined without destroying the object. For example, color, shape, mass, length, density, specific heat and odor are all examples of physical properties.

A chemical property indicates how a substance reacts with something else. When a chemical property is observed, the original substance is changed into a different substance. For example, the ability of iron to rust is a chemical property. The iron has reacted with oxygen and the original iron metal is gone. It is now iron oxide, a new substance. All chemical changes include physical changes.

Classify the following properties as either chemical or physical by putting a check in the appropriate column.

	Physical Property	Chemical Property
1. red color		
2. density		
3. flammability		
4. solubility		
5. reacts with acid to form hydrogen		
6. supports combustion		
7. bitter taste		
8. melting point		
9. reacts with water to form a gas		
10. reacts with a base to form water		
11. hardness		
12. boiling point		
13. can neutralize a base		
14. luster		
15. odor		

PHYSICAL VS. CHEMICAL CHANGE

Name _____

In a physical change, the original substance still exists, it has only changed in form. Energy changes usually do not accompany physical changes, except in phase changes and when substances dissolve.

In a chemical change, a new substance is produced. Energy changes always accompany chemical changes. Chemical changes are always accompanied by physical changes.

Classify the following as examples of a physical change, a chemical change or both kinds of change.

1. Sodium hydroxide dissolves in water. _____

2. Hydrochloric acid reacts with sodium hydroxide to produce a salt, water and heat. _____

3. A pellet of sodium is sliced in two. _____

4. Water is heated and changed to steam. _____

5. Potassium chlorate decomposes to potassium chloride and oxygen gas. _____

6. Iron rusts. _____

7. Ice melts. _____

8. Acid on limestone produces carbon dioxide gas. _____

9. Milk sours. _____

10. Wood rots. _____

SEPARATION OF MIXTURES

Name _____

Taking advantage of various physical and chemical properties, how would you separate the following mixtures into their components?

1. Sand and water _____

   _____

   _____

2. Sugar and water _____

   _____

   _____

3. Oil and water _____

   _____

   _____

4. Sand and gravel _____

   _____

   _____

5. A mixture of heptane (boiling point 98°C) and heptanol (boiling point 176°C)

   _____

   _____

6. A mixture of iodine solid and sodium chloride (Hint: Iodine is not soluble in water.)

   _____

   _____

   _____

7. A mixture of lead and aluminum pellets_____

   _____

   _____

8. A mixture of salt and iron filings _____

   _____

   _____

STATES OF MATTER CROSSWORD

Name _____

ACROSS

3. Change of a gas to a liquid
6. This type of property can be observed without destroying the substance.
7. Mass of a substance divided by unit volume
8. Physical change of a solid to a liquid at the melting point
9. State of matter having no definite volume or shape
10. Homogeneous mixture
12. This type of change produces a new substance.
13. Change of a liquid to a solid

DOWN

1. Anything that has mass and takes up space
2. State in which atoms or molecules are very close together and are regularly arranged
4. Change of a liquid to a gas
5. This state of matter consists of electrically charged particles.
10. Elements and compounds
11. State of matter having a definite volume but no definite shape.

ELEMENTS AND THEIR SYMBOLS

Name _____

Write the symbols for the following elements.

1. oxygen _____
2. hydrogen _____
3. chlorine _____
4. sodium _____
5. fluorine _____
6. carbon _____
7. helium _____
8. nitrogen _____
9. copper _____
10. sulfur _____

11. magnesium _____
12. manganese _____
13. neon _____
14. bromine _____
15. phosphorus _____
16. silver _____
17. lead _____
18. iron _____
19. calcium _____
20. potassium _____

Write the name of the element that corresponds to each of the following symbols.

21. Cu _____
22. K _____
23. C _____
24. Au _____
25. Zn _____
26. Pb _____
27. Fe _____
28. Na _____
29. S _____
30. Al _____

31. Ca _____
32. Ag _____
33. P _____
34. O _____
35. I _____
36. Sn _____
37. H _____
38. F _____
39. Ni _____
40. Hg _____

ELEMENTS CROSSWORD

Name _____

ACROSS

2. Element on which life is based

4. Its low melting point is useful in automatic sprinkler systems.

6. Its common allotropes are red and white.

11. It is a good conductor.

12. Halogen found in seawater

13. Most abundant halogen

14. Gas used in lighted signs to produce a red color

DOWN

1. Most abundant element in air

3. Fire resistant material no longer used due to its carcinogenicity

5. Light element used for lifting airships

7. Ozone is an allotrope of this element.

8. This element is responsible for the odor of rotten eggs.

9. Poisonous element that is also used in medicines and rat poison

10. Most reactive nonmetal

PARTS OF AN ATOM

An atom is made up of protons and neutrons which are in the nucleus, and electrons which are in the electron cloud surrounding the atom.

The atomic number equals the number of protons. The electrons in a neutral atom equal the number of protons. The mass number equals the sum of the protons and neutrons.

The charge indicates the number of electrons that have been lost or gained. A positive charge indicates the number of electrons (which are negatively charged) lost.
A negative charge indicates the number of electrons gained.

This structure can be written as part of a chemical symbol.

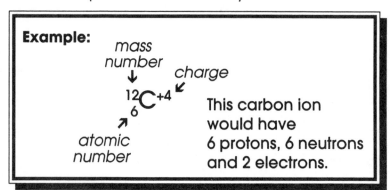

Example:

mass number

charge

$^{12}_{6}C^{+4}$

atomic number

This carbon ion would have 6 protons, 6 neutrons and 2 electrons.

Complete the following chart.

Element/ Ion	Atomic Number	Mass Number	Charge	Protons	Neutrons	Electrons
$^{24}_{12}Mg$						
$^{39}_{19}K$						
$^{23}_{11}Na^{+1}$						
$^{19}_{9}F^{-1}$						
$^{27}_{13}Al^{+3}$						
$^{1}_{1}H$						
$^{24}Mg^{2+}$						
Ag						
S^{-2}						
$^{2}_{1}H$						
$^{35}Cl^{-}$						
Be^{2+}						

BOHR MODELS

Name _____

Draw Bohr models of the following atoms.

1. $^{1}_{1}H$	2. $^{4}_{2}He$
3. $^{7}_{3}Li$	4. $^{23}_{11}Na$
5. $^{35}_{17}Cl$	6. $^{64}_{29}Cu$

PROPERTIES OF METALS AND NONMETALS

Name _____

For the following physical and chemical properties, put a check in the appropriate column if it applies to a metal or a nonmetal.

Property	Metal	Nonmetal
1. malleable		
2. lustrous		
3. gaseous at room temperature		
4. forms negative ions		
5. metallic bonding		
6. more than 4 valence electrons		
7. conducts electricity in solid state		
8. ductile		
9. brittle		
10. only forms positive ions		
11. nonconductor		
12. covalent bonding		
13. can have both positive and negative oxidation numbers		
14. gives away electrons in chemical reactions		
15. prefers to receive electrons in chemical reactions		

ACTIVITY OF THE ELEMENTS

Name _____

Since metals prefer to give away electrons during chemical bonding, the most active metals are closest to francium, which is a large atom with low ionization energy and electronegativity. Nonmetals prefer to pull in electrons, so the most active nonmetals are closest to fluorine, which has a high ionization energy and electronegativity. The noble gases (Group 18) are considered inactive since they already have a stable octet of electrons in their outer shell.

Referring to a periodic table, circle the member of each pair of elements which is most chemically active.

1.   Li and Na

2. Cl_2 and F_2

3. N_2 and Ne

4.   Rb and Ca

5.   Ti and Ca

6.   K and Mg

7. O_2 and S

8. I_2 and Br_2

9.   Na and Zn

10.   P and S

11. N_2 and O_2

12. Cl_2 and Ar

13.   Ba and Fr

14.   Rb and Cu

15.   Be and Cr

16. Cl_2 and Br_2

17.   Xe and I_2

18.   Fe and Ra

19.   Sr and Mn

20.   K and Na

21.   Au and Mg

22.   S and Rn

23.   Li and Be

24.   Se and Br_2

25. I_2 and F_2

26.   Rb and Sr

27.   Ba and Ra

28.   Na and Mg

29.   Te and I_2

30.   Ca and Rn

PERIODIC TABLE PUZZLE

Name _____

Group Number

1	2	3	4	5	6	7	8	9	10	11	12	13	14	15	16	17	18
I																	
	F														G	H	
													B				A
C							E				J						

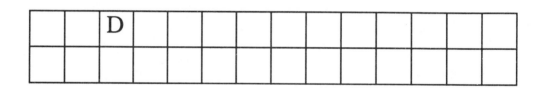

Place the letter of each of the above elements next to its description below. Each answer may be used only once, so choose the best answer in each case.

1. An alkali metal ____

2. An alkaline earth metal ____

3. An inactive gas ____

4. An active nonmetal ____

5. A semimetal ____

6. An inner transition element ____

7. Its most common oxidation state is -2. ____

8. A metal with more than one oxidation state ____

9. Metal with an oxidation number of +3 ____

10. Has oxidation numbers of +1 and -1 ____

PERIODIC TABLE CROSSWORD

Name _____

Across

2. Group I metals
4. Elements in the middle of the periodic table are the ____ metals.
5. The sum of the protons and neutrons is the ____ number.
6. Inactive gases.
7. The horizontal rows are called ____ .
8. Most of the elements are ____ .
10. Nonmetals tend to form ____ ions.

Down

1. Most active nonmetals
2. Group II metals
3. Atomic number is the number of ____ .
7. Metals tend to form ____ ions.
9. The elements are arranged by atomic ____ .
11. The vertical columns are called families or ____ .

TYPES OF CHEMICAL BONDS

Name _____

Classify the following compounds as ionic (metal and nonmetal), covalent (nonmetal and nonmetal) or both (compound containing a polyatomic ion).

1. $CaCl_2$ _____

2. CO_2 _____

3. H_2O _____

4. $BaSO_4$ _____

5. K_2O _____

6. NaF _____

7. Na_2CO_3 _____

8. CH_4 _____

9. SO_3 _____

10. LiBr _____

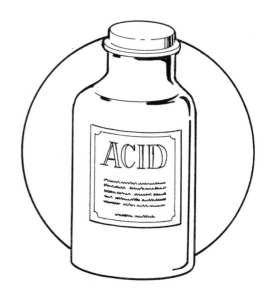

11. MgO _____

12. NH_4Cl _____

13. HCl _____

14. KI _____

15. NaOH _____

16. NO_2 _____

17. $AlPO_4$ _____

18. $FeCl_3$ _____

19. P_2O_5 _____

20. N_2O_3 _____

NUMBER OF ATOMS IN A FORMULA

Name _____

Determine the number of atoms in the following chemical formulas.

1. NaCl _____

2. H_2SO_4 _____

3. KNO_3 _____

4. $CaCl_2$ _____

5. C_2H_6 _____

6. $Ba(OH)_2$ _____

7. NH_4Br _____

8. $Ca_3(PO_4)_2$ _____

9. $Al_2(SO_4)_3$ _____

10. $Mg(NO_3)_2$ _____

11. $Cu(NO_3)_2$ _____

12. $KMnO_4$ _____

13. H_2O_2 _____

14. H_3PO_4 _____

15. $(NH_4)_3PO_4$ _____

16. Fe_2O_3 _____

17. $NaC_2H_3O_2$ _____

18. $Mg(C_2H_3O_2)_2$ _____

19. Hg_2Cl_2 _____

20. K_2SO_3 _____

GRAM FORMULA MASS

Name _____

Determine the gram formula mass of each of the following compounds.

1. NaCl _____

2. H_2SO_4 _____

3. KNO_3 _____

4. $CaCl_2$ _____

5. C_2H_6 _____

6. $Ba(OH)_2$ _____

7. NH_4Br _____

8. $Ca_3(PO_4)_2$ _____

9. $Al_2(SO_4)_3$ _____

10. $Mg(NO_3)_2$ _____

11. $Cu(NO_3)_2$ _____

12. $KMnO_4$ _____

13. H_2O_2 _____

14. H_3PO_4 _____

15. $(NH_4)_3PO_4$ _____

16. Fe_2O_3 _____

17. $NaC_2H_3O_2$ _____

18. $Mg(C_2H_3O_2)_2$ _____

19. Hg_2Cl_2 _____

20. K_2SO_3 _____

PERCENTAGE COMPOSITION

Name _____

Solve the following problems.

1. What is the percentage of carbon in CO_2?

   Answer: _____

2. How many grams of carbon are in 25 g of CO_2?

   Answer: _____

3. What is the percentage of sodium in NaCl?

   Answer: _____

4. How many grams of sodium are in 75 g of NaCl?

   Answer: _____

5. What is the percentage of oxygen in $KClO_3$?

   Answer: _____

6. How many grams of oxygen can be obtained from 5.00 g of $KClO_3$?

   Answer: _____

7. What is the percentage of silver in $AgNO_3$?

   Answer: _____

8. How many grams of silver can be recovered from 125 g of $AgNO_3$?

   Answer: _____

9. What is the percentage of gold in $AuCl_3$?

   Answer: _____

10. How many grams of gold can be recovered from 35.0 g of $AuCl_3$?

    Answer: _____

WRITING BINARY FORMULAS

Name _____

Write the formulas for the compounds formed from the following ions.

1. Na^+, Cl^- _____

2. Ba^{+2}, F^- _____

3. K^+, S^{-2} _____

4. Li^+, Br^- _____

5. Al^{+3}, I^- _____

6. Zn^{+2}, S^{-2} _____

7. Ag^+, O^{-2} _____

8. Mg^{+2}, P^{-3} _____

9. Ni^{+2}, O^{-2} _____

10. Ni^{+3}, O^{-2} _____

11. Fe^{+2}, O^{-2} _____

12. Fe^{+3}, O^{-2} _____

13. Cr^{+2}, S^{-2} _____

14. Cr^{+3}, S^{-2} _____

15. Cu^+, Cl^- _____

16. Cu^{+2}, Cl^- _____

17. Pb^{+2}, O^{-2} _____

18. Pb^{+4}, O^{-2} _____

19. Mn^{+2}, Br^- _____

20. Mn^{+4}, Br^- _____

NAMING BINARY COMPOUNDS (IONIC)

Name _____

Name the following ionic compounds using Roman numerals where necessary.

1. $BaCl_2$ _____

2. NaF _____

3. Ag_2O _____

4. $CuBr$ _____

5. $CuBr_2$ _____

6. FeO _____

7. Fe_2O_3 _____

8. MgS _____

9. Al_2O_3 _____

10. CaI_2 _____

11. K_2S _____

12. $CrCl_2$ _____

13. $CrCl_3$ _____

14. CaO _____

15. Ba_3P_2 _____

16. Hg_2I_2 _____

17. Na_2O _____

18. BeS _____

19. MnO _____

20. Mn_2O_3 _____

NAMING BINARY COMPOUNDS (COVALENT)

Name _____

Name the following compounds using the prefix method.

1. CO _____

2. CO_2 _____

3. SO_2 _____

4. NO_2 _____

5. N_2O _____

6. SO_3 _____

7. CCl_4 _____

8. NO _____

9. N_2O_5 _____

10. P_2O_5 _____

11. N_2O_4 _____

12. CS_2 _____

13. OF_2 _____

14. PCl_3 _____

15. PBr_5 _____

FORMULAS WITH POLYATOMIC IONS

Name _____

Matching the horizontal and vertical axes, write the formulas of the compounds with the following combination of ions. The first one is done for you.

	OH^-	NO_3^-	CO_3^{-2}	SO_4^{-2}	PO_4^{-3}
H^+	HOH (H_2O)	HNO_3	H_2CO_3	H_2SO_4	H_3PO_4
Na^+					
Mg^{+2}					
NH_4^+					
Ca^{+2}					
K^+					
Al^{+3}					
Pb^{+4}					

NAMING OF NON-BINARY COMPOUNDS

Name _____

An ionic compound that contains more than two elements must contain a polyatomic ion. Name the following compounds.

1. $NaNO_3$ _____

2. $Ca(OH)_2$ _____

3. K_2CO_3 _____

4. NH_4Cl _____

5. $MgSO_4$ _____

6. $AlPO_4$ _____

7. $(NH_4)_2SO_4$ _____

8. Na_3PO_4 _____

9. $CuSO_4$ _____

10. NH_4OH _____

11. Li_2SO_3 _____

12. $Mg(NO_3)_2$ _____

13. $Al(OH)_3$ _____

14. $(NH_4)_3PO_4$ _____

15. KOH _____

16. $Ca(NO_3)_2$ _____

17. K_2SO_4 _____

18. $Pb(OH)_2$ _____

19. Na_2O_2 _____

20. $CuCO_3$ _____

NAMING COMPOUNDS (MIXED)

Name _____

Name the following compounds.

1. $NaCl$ _____

2. MnS _____

3. K_2O _____

4. $CuBr_2$ _____

5. $CuBr$ _____

6. CO_2 _____

7. $PbSO_4$ _____

8. Li_2CO_3 _____

9. Na_2CO_3 _____

10. NO_2 _____

11. N_2O_4 _____

12. $Ca(OH)_2$ _____

13. NH_4Cl _____

14. SO_3 _____

15. $AlPO_4$ _____

16. CCl_4 _____

17. CaS _____

18. NH_3 _____

19. MgI_2 _____

20. K_3PO_4 _____

WRITING FORMULAS FROM NAMES

Name _____

Write the formulas for the following compounds.

1. carbon monoxide _____

2. sodium chloride _____

3. carbon tetrachloride _____

4. magnesium bromide _____

5. aluminum iodide _____

6. hydrogen hydroxide _____

7. iron (II) fluoride _____

8. carbon dioxide _____

9. sodium carbonate _____

10. ammonium sulfide _____

11. iron (II) oxide _____

12. iron (III) oxide _____

13. magnesium sulfate _____

14. sodium phosphate _____

15. dinitrogen pentoxide _____

16. phosphorus trichloride _____

17. aluminum sulfite _____

18. copper (I) carbonate _____

19. potassium hydrogen carbonate _____

20. sulfur trioxide _____

BALANCING EQUATIONS

Name _____

Balance the following chemical equations.

1. $CH_4 + O_2 \rightarrow CO_2 + H_2O$

2. $Na + I_2 \rightarrow NaI$

3. $N_2 + O_2 \rightarrow N_2O$

4. $N_2 + H_2 \rightarrow NH_3$

5. $KI + Cl_2 \rightarrow KCl + I_2$

6. $HCl + Ca(OH)_2 \rightarrow CaCl_2 + H_2O$

7. $KClO_3 \rightarrow KCl + O_2$

8. $K_3PO_4 + HCl \rightarrow KCl + H_3PO_4$

9. $S + O_2 \rightarrow SO_3$

10. $KI + Pb(NO_3)_2 \rightarrow KNO_3 + PbI_2$

11. $CaSO_4 + AlBr_3 \rightarrow CaBr_2 + Al_2(SO_4)_3$

12. $H_2O_2 \rightarrow H_2O + O_2$

13. $Na + H_2O \rightarrow NaOH + H_2$

14. $C_2H_6 + O_2 \rightarrow CO_2 + H_2O$

15. $Mg(NO_3)_2 + K_3PO_4 \rightarrow Mg_3(PO_4)_2 + KNO_3$

WORD EQUATIONS

Name _____

Write and balance the following chemical equations.

1. Hydrogen plus oxygen yield water.

2. Nitrogen plus hydrogen yield ammonia.

3. Aluminum bromide plus chlorine yield aluminum chloride and bromine.

4. Hydrochloric acid plus sodium hydroxide yield sodium chloride plus water.

5. Iron plus lead (II) sulfate react forming iron (II) sulfate plus lead.

6. Potassium chlorate when heated produces potassium chloride plus oxygen gas.

7. Sulfuric acid decomposes to form sulfur trioxide gas plus water.

8. Sodium oxide combines with water to make sodium hydroxide.

9. Potassium iodide reacts with bromine forming potassium bromide plus iodine.

10. Sodium phosphate reacts with calcium nitrate to produce sodium nitrate plus calcium phosphate.

11. Zinc reacts with iron (III) chloride yielding zinc chloride plus iron precipitate.

12. Ammonium carbonate and magnesium sulfate react to yield ammonium sulfate plus magnesium carbonate.

13. Phosphoric acid plus calcium hydroxide react forming solid calcium phosphate plus water.

14. Aluminum plus oxygen gas form aluminum oxide under certain conditions.

15. Nitrogen gas plus oxygen gas react and form dinitrogen pentoxide.

CLASSIFYING CHEMICAL REACTIONS Name _____

Classify the following reactions as synthesis, decomposition, single replacement or double replacement.

1. $2KClO_3 \rightarrow 2KCl + 3O_2$

2. $HCl + NaOH \rightarrow NaCl + H_2O$

3. $Mg + 2HCl \rightarrow MgCl_2 + H_2$

4. $2H_2 + O_2 \rightarrow 2H_2O$

5. $2Al + 3NiBr_2 \rightarrow 2AlBr_3 + 3Ni$

6. $4Al + 3O_2 \rightarrow 2Al_2O_3$

7. $2NaCl \rightarrow 2Na + Cl_2$

8. $CaCl_2 + F_2 \rightarrow CaF_2 + Cl_2$

9. $AgNO_3 + KCl \rightarrow AgCl + KNO_3$

10. $N_2 + 3H_2 \rightarrow 2NH_3$

11. $2H_2O_2 \rightarrow 2H_2O + O_2$

12. $(NH_4)_2SO_4 + Ba(NO_3)_2 \rightarrow BaSO_4 + 2NH_4NO_3$

13. $MgI_2 + Br_2 \rightarrow MgBr_2 + I_2$

14. $SO_3 + H_2O \rightarrow H_2SO_4$

15. $6KCl + Zn_3(PO_4)_2 \rightarrow 3ZnCl_2 + 2K_3PO_4$

CONSERVATION OF MASS

Name _____

In chemical reactions, mass is neither gained nor lost. The total mass of all the reactants equals the total mass of all the products. Atoms are just rearranged into different compounds.

Using this idea, solve the following problems.

1. $2KClO_3 \rightarrow 2KCl + 3O_2$

   If 500 g of $KClO_3$ decomposes and produces 303 g of KCl, how many grams of O_2 are produced?

   _____

2. $N_2 + 3H_2 \rightarrow 2NH_3$

   How many grams of H_2 are needed to react with 100 g of N_2 to produce 121 g of NH_3?

   _____

3. $4Fe + 3O_2 \rightarrow 2Fe_2O_3$

   How many grams of oxygen are needed to react with 350 g of iron to produce 500 g of Fe_2O_3?

   _____

4. $CH_4 + 2O_2 \rightarrow CO_2 + 2H_2O$

   16 g of CH_4 react with 64 g of O_2, producing 44 g of CO_2. How many grams of water are produced?

   _____

5. $CaCO_3 \rightarrow CaO + CO_2$

   How much CO_2 is produced from the decomposition of 200 g of $CaCO_3$ if 112 g of CaO are produced?

   _____

MASS RELATIONSHIPS IN EQUATIONS Name _____

A balanced equation can tell us the mass relationships involved in a chemical reaction.

Example 1: $2KClO_3 \rightarrow 2KCl + 3O_2$

How many grams of KCl are produced if 244 g of $KClO_3$ decompose?

Solution: 1 formula mass of $KClO_3$ = 122 g
1 formula mass of KCl = 74 g

$$244 \text{ g } KClO_3 \times \frac{2(74 \text{ g) KCl}}{2(122 \text{ g) } KClO_3} = 148 \text{ g KCl}$$

coefficients from equation

Example 2: $N_2 + 3H_2 \rightarrow 2NH_3$

How many grams of H_2 are needed to react with 56 g of N_2?

Solution: 1 formula mass of N_2 = 28 g
1 formula mass of H_2 = 2 g

$$56 \text{ g } N_2 \times \frac{3(2 \text{ g) } H_2}{1(28 \text{ g)} N_2} = 12 \text{ g}$$

Solve the following problems.

1. $2H_2O_2 \rightarrow 2H_2O + O_2$

How many grams of water are produced from the decomposition of 68 g of H_2O_2?

_____

2. How many grams of oxygen are produced in the above reaction?

_____

3. $2C_2H_6 + 7O_2 \rightarrow 4CO_2 + 6H_2O$

How many grams of oxygen are required to completely react with 120 g of C_2H_6?

_____

4. How many grams of CO_2 are produced in the above reaction?

_____

5. $2K_3PO_4 + 3MgCl_2 \rightarrow Mg_3(PO_4)_2 + 6KCl$

How much $MgCl_2$ is required to react exactly with 500 g of K_3PO_4?

_____

6. How much KCl will be produced in the above reaction?

_____

65

ACID, BASE OR SALT

Name _____

Classify each of the following compounds as an acid, base or salt. Then, indicate whether each acid and base is strong or weak.

1. HNO_3 _____   _____

2. $NaOH$ _____   _____

3. $NaNO_3$ _____   _____

4. HCl _____   _____

5. KCl _____   _____

6. $Ba(OH)_2$ _____   _____

7. KOH _____   _____

8. H_2S _____   _____

9. $Al(NO_3)_3$ _____   _____

10. H_2SO_4 _____   _____

11. $CaCl_2$ _____   _____

12. H_3PO_4 _____   _____

13. Na_2SO_4 _____   _____

14. $Mg(OH)_2$ _____   _____

15. H_2CO_3 _____   _____

16. NH_4OH _____   _____

17. NH_4Cl _____   _____

18. HBr _____   _____

19. $FeBr_3$ _____   _____

20. HF _____   _____

pH

pH is a scale that measures the hydronium ion concentration of a solution. Therefore, the pH scale can be used to determine the acidity of a solution. A pH of less than 7 indicates an acidic solution, a pH of 7 is neutral, and a pH of greater than 7 up to 14 is basic. The lower the pH, the higher the acidity. The higher the pH, the lower the acidity.

Indicators are substances that change color at a different pH levels. Phenolphthalein is colorless in an acid and a neutral solution, pink in a base. Blue litmus changes to red in an acid, and remains blue in neutral and basic solutions. Red litmus remains red in acidic and neutral substances, but turns blue in bases.

Complete the following chart.

pH	Acid, Base, Neutral	Phenolphthalein	Blue Litmus	Red Litmus
2				
8				
4				
7				
13				
11				
5				
1				

pH OF SALT SOLUTIONS

Name _____

A salt is formed from the reaction of an acid and a base.

   A strong acid + a strong base → neutral salt

   A strong acid + a weak base → acidic salt

   A weak acid + a strong base → basic salt

The salt of a weak acid and a weak base may be acidic, neutral or basic, depending on the relative strengths of the acids and bases involved.

The strong acids are HI, HBr, HCl, HNO_3, H_2SO_4 and $HClO_4$. The strong bases are the Group I and Group II hydroxides. Most others are considered weak.

Complete the following chart. The first one is done for you.

Salt	Parent Acid	Acid Strength	Parent Base	Base Strength	Type of Salt
KBr	HBr	Strong	KOH	Strong	Neutral
$Fe(NO_3)_2$					
NaF					
NH_4Cl					
$Ca(NO_3)_2$					
Li_3PO_4					
K_2SO_4					
AlI_3					
$MgCO_3$					
$Zn(ClO_4)_2$					

68

CONDUCTORS AND ELECTROLYTES

Name _____

Pure metals are good conductors of electricity. Electrolytes are aqueous solutions that conduct electricity. Acids, bases and salts (ionic compounds) are electrolytes. Nonelectrolytes are aqueous solutions that do not conduct electricity. The solutes used to form nonelectrolytes are covalently bonded.

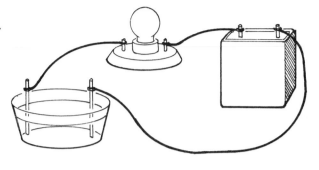

Classify the following as conductors or nonconductors by writing C or N next to each.

1. copper _____

2. hydrogen _____

3. NaOH(aq) _____

4. NaCl(s) _____

5. NaCl(aq) _____

6. magnesium _____

7. H_2SO_4 _____

8. NH_4OH _____

9. HCl(aq) _____

10. $Ca(OH)_2$(aq) _____

11. $C_6H_{12}O_6$(aq) _____

12. CH_3OH _____

13. KNO_3(s) _____

14. KNO_3(aq) _____

15. chlorine _____

16. HNO_3 _____

17. $NaNO_3$(aq) _____

18. $C_{12}H_{22}O_{11}$ _____

19. C_2H_5OH _____

20. gold _____

EFFECT OF DISSOLVED PARTICLES ON FREEZING AND BOILING POINTS

Name _____

The graph below shows a time/temperature graph for the heating of water. Directly on the graph, sketch the approximate curve that would result when

a) 5 g of sugar ($C_6H_{12}O_6$) are dissolved in the sample;

b) 5 g of NaCl are dissolved;

c) 10g of NaCl are dissolved.

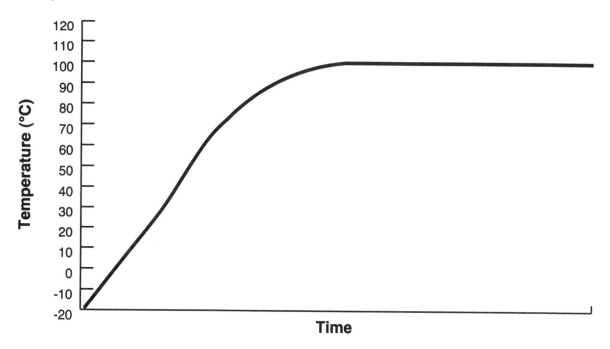

Do the same on the graph below for solutions a, b and c when the solution is cooled through its freezing point.

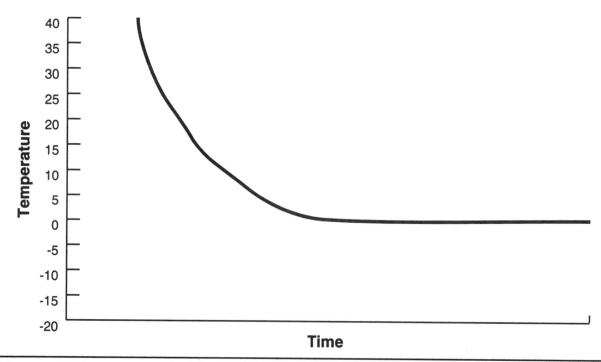

CONCENTRATION (MASS/VOLUME)

Name _____

$$\text{Concentration} = \frac{\text{mass of solute}}{\text{volume of solution}}$$

Solve the following problems.

1. A sugar solution contains 26 g of sugar in 0.50 L of solution. What is the concentration in g/L?

   _____

2. 45 grams of salt are dissolved in 0.10 L of solution. What is the concentration in g/L?

   _____

3. A solution contains 25 g of sugar per liter of solution. How many grams of sugar are in 1.5 L of solution?

   _____

4. A solution contains 85 g of corn syrup per liter of solution. How many grams of corn syrup are in 500 mL of solution?

   _____

5. How many liters of salt solution would be needed to provide 30 g of salt if the concentration of the solution is 20 g/L?

   _____

CONCENTRATION (% BY VOLUME)

Name _____

$$\% \text{ volume} = \frac{V_{solute}}{V_{total}} \times 100\%$$

Solve the following problems. Assume all volumes are additive.

1. 25 mL of ethanol is added to enough water to make 100 mL of solution. Find the percent by volume of ethanol.

   _____

2. 50 mL of ethanol is added to 50 mL of water. What is the percent by volume of ethanol?

   _____

3. 3.0 liters of antifreeze is added to 4.0 liters of water. Find the percent by volume of antifreeze.

   _____

4. A popular fruit drink contains 5% by volume fruit juice. How much fruit juice is in 500 mL of the fruit drink?

   _____

5. How much corn syrup should be added to water to make 200 mL of a 10% by volume solution?

   _____

CONCENTRATION (% BY MASS)

Name _____

$$\text{Concentration} = \frac{\text{mass of solute}}{\text{mass of solution}} \times 100\%$$

Solve the following problems.

1. 25 g of sugar in 75 g of solution will have what percent by mass of sugar?

   _____

2. 35 g of salt is dissolved in 500 g of total solution. What is the percent by mass of salt?

   _____

3. 50 g of sugar are dissolved in 50 g of water. What is the percent by mass of sugar?

   _____

4. 75 g of potassium nitrate are dissolved in 150 g of water. What is the percent by mass of potassium nitrate?

   _____

5. How many grams of sodium bromide are in 200 g of a solution that is 15% sodium bromide by mass?

   _____

73

SOLUBILITY

Name _____

Classify the following compounds as soluble or insoluble following the rules for solubility.

1. $AgNO_3$ _____

2. K_2CO_3 _____

3. $Ca_3(PO_4)_2$ _____

4. $AgCl$ _____

5. $NaOH$ _____

6. NH_4Cl _____

7. KBr _____

8. $MgCO_3$ _____

9. FeS _____

10. $CuC_2H_3O_2$ _____

11. $(NH_4)_2SO_4$ _____

12. $Ca(OH)_2$ _____

13. Na_2SO_4 _____

14. $BaSO_4$ _____

15. KI _____

16. $(NH_4)_3PO_4$ _____

17. $Cu(NO_3)_2$ _____

18. $AlPO_4$ _____

19. $CaCO_3$ _____

20. $(NH_4)_2S$ _____

NAMING ORGANIC COMPOUNDS

Name _____

Name the following organic compounds.

1. $$\begin{array}{c} H \\ | \\ H - C - H \\ | \\ H \end{array}$$	**5.** $$\begin{array}{c} H \quad H \quad H \quad H \\ | \quad\; | \quad\; | \quad\; | \\ H - C = C - C - C - H \\ \qquad\quad | \quad\; | \\ \qquad\quad H \quad H \end{array}$$
2. $$\begin{array}{c} H \quad H \quad H \\ | \quad\; | \quad\; | \\ H - C = C - C - H \\ \qquad\qquad | \\ \qquad\qquad H \end{array}$$	**6.** $$\begin{array}{c} H \quad H \quad H \\ | \quad\; | \quad\; | \\ H - C - C - C - H \\ | \quad\; | \quad\; | \\ H \quad H \quad H \end{array}$$
3. $$H - C \equiv C - H$$	**7.** $$\begin{array}{c} H \\ | \\ H - C \equiv C - C - H \\ | \\ H \end{array}$$
4. $$\begin{array}{c} H \quad H \\ | \quad\; | \\ H - C - C - H \\ | \quad\; | \\ H \quad H \end{array}$$	**8.** $$\begin{array}{c} H \quad H \\ | \quad\; | \\ H - C = C - H \end{array}$$

DRAWING STRUCTURAL FORMULAS

Name _____

Draw the structural formula of the following compounds.

1. ethane	5. propyne
2. propene	6. methane
3. 1-butyne	7. ethyne
4. ethene	8. 1-pentene

ISOMERS

Name _____

Isomers have the same chemical formula but different structural formulas. Match the structure in Column I with its isomer in Column II.

I

II

1.

$$H - \underset{\underset{H}{|}}{\overset{\overset{H}{|}}{C}} - \underset{\underset{H}{|}}{\overset{\overset{H}{|}}{C}} - \underset{\underset{H}{|}}{\overset{\overset{H}{|}}{C}} - OH$$

_____

a)

$$H - \underset{\underset{H}{|}}{\overset{\overset{H}{|}}{C}} - \underset{\underset{H}{|}}{\overset{\overset{CH_3}{|}}{C}} - \underset{\underset{H}{|}}{\overset{\overset{H}{|}}{C}} - H$$

2.

$$H - \underset{\underset{H}{|}}{\overset{\overset{H}{|}}{C}} - \overset{\overset{O}{||}}{C} - \underset{\underset{H}{|}}{\overset{\overset{H}{|}}{C}} - H$$

_____

b)

$$H - \underset{\underset{H}{|}}{\overset{\overset{H}{|}}{C}} - \underset{\underset{H}{|}}{\overset{\overset{OH}{|}}{C}} - \underset{\underset{H}{|}}{\overset{\overset{H}{|}}{C}} - H$$

3.

$$H - \underset{\underset{H}{|}}{\overset{\overset{H}{|}}{C}} - \underset{\underset{H}{|}}{\overset{\overset{H}{|}}{C}} - \underset{\underset{H}{|}}{\overset{\overset{H}{|}}{C}} - \underset{\underset{H}{|}}{\overset{\overset{H}{|}}{C}} - H$$

_____

c)

$$H_3C - \underset{\underset{CH_3}{|}}{\overset{\overset{CH_3}{|}}{C}} - CH_3$$

4.

$$H - \underset{\underset{H}{|}}{\overset{\overset{H}{|}}{C}} - \underset{\underset{H}{|}}{\overset{\overset{H}{|}}{C}} - \underset{\underset{H}{|}}{\overset{\overset{H}{|}}{C}} - \underset{\underset{H}{|}}{\overset{\overset{H}{|}}{C}} - \underset{\underset{H}{|}}{\overset{\overset{H}{|}}{C}} - H$$

_____

d)

$$H - \underset{\underset{H}{|}}{\overset{\overset{H}{|}}{C}} - \underset{\underset{H}{|}}{\overset{\overset{H}{|}}{C}} - \overset{\overset{O}{||}}{C} - H$$

5.

$$H - \underset{\underset{H}{|}}{\overset{\overset{H}{|}}{C}} - \overset{\overset{O}{||}}{C} - OH$$

_____

e)

$$H - \underset{\underset{H}{|}}{\overset{\overset{H}{|}}{C}} - O - \overset{\overset{O}{||}}{C} - H$$

ORGANIC CHEMISTRY CROSSWORD

Name _____

Across

4. Compound containing only carbon and hydrogen
6. Produced when one or more of the hydrogens in a hydrocarbon is replaced by a hydroxyl group
7. All carbon atoms are joined by single covalent bonds
8. Sugar and starch
9. Long chains of carbon atoms produced by joining small chains together
10. Ingredient of gasoline

Down

1. Compounds with the same chemical formula but different structures
2. Organic compounds in the body used to store energy
3. Compound containing a double or triple covalent bond
5. Polymer made from smaller molecules called amino acids
9. Mixture of hydrocarbons that are used for fuels

WAVE DIAGRAM

Name _____

On the following diagram, place the following terms in their correct places: amplitude, wavelength, crest, trough, rest position.

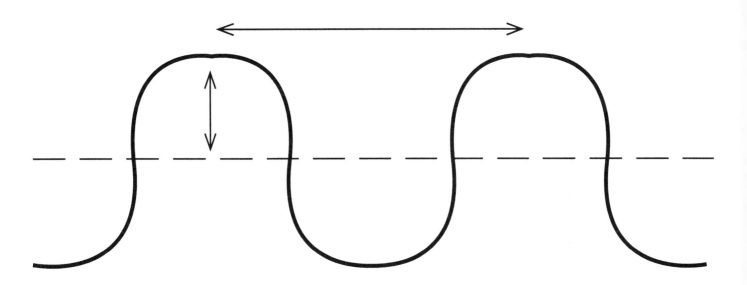

Define the terms below.

amplitude _____

_____

wavelength _____

_____

crest _____

_____

trough _____

_____

WAVE VELOCITY CALCULATIONS

Name _____

Solve the following problems.

1. A tuning fork has a frequency of 280 hertz, and the wavelength of the sound produced is 1.5 meters. Calculate the velocity of the wave.

_____

2. A wave is moving toward shore with a velocity of 5.0 m/s. If its frequency is 2.5 hertz, what is its wavelength?

_____

3. The speed of light is 3.0×10^8 m/s. Red light has a wavelength of 7×10^{-7} m. What is its frequency?

_____

4. The frequency of violet light is 7.5×10^{14} hertz. What is its wavelength?

_____

5. A jump rope is shaken producing a wave with a wavelength of 0.5 m with the crest of the wave passing a certain point 4 times per second. What is the velocity of the wave?

_____

SOUND AND MUSIC CROSSWORD

Name _____

Across

3. Has a higher frequency than the fundamental frequency

5. The control of noise and the vibrations that cause noise

7. The lowest frequency in a musical sound

9. Type of wave in which matter vibrates in the same direction that the wave travels

11. Eight notes on the musical scale

13. As the amplitude of sound waves increases, the _____ of the sound increases.

14. Area where sound waves are pushed together

15. The combination of two or more sound waves can cause _____ .

Down

1. Sound does not travel through a _____ .

2. This effect is a change in wave frequency caused by the motion of the source of the wave.

4. Area where sound waves are pushed apart

6. Produced when overtones have frequencies that are whole number multiples of the fundamental

8. Sounds that cannot be heard by human beings

10. This depends on the frequency of the sound waves.

12. The intensity of sounds are measured in units called _____ .

REFLECTION

Draw the expected path of the light rays as they reflect off the following plane mirrors.

1.

2.

3.

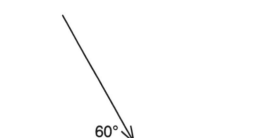

4.

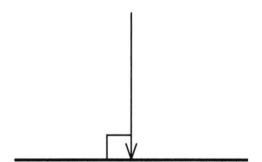

5.

6.

REFRACTION

Draw the pathway of the light beam as it passes through each of the following substances. Using a protractor, measure the refracted angle.

1.

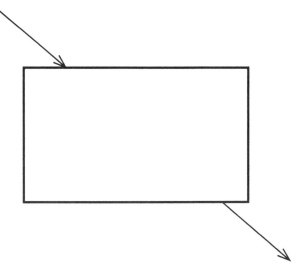

Which substance has the greatest

index of refraction? _____

2.

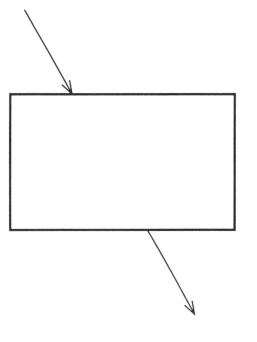

3.

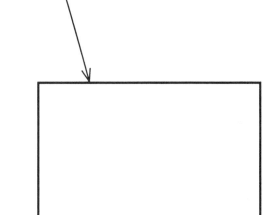

LIGHT RAYS AND CONVEX LENSES

Name _____

Draw the pathways of the light from the objects on the left through the convex lenses. Label the focal point and the inverted image.

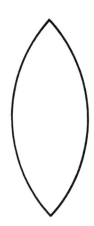

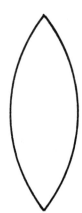

LIGHT RAYS AND CONCAVE LENSES

Draw the path of light through the concave lenses below. Label the image and focal point.

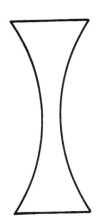

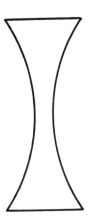

85

WHITE LIGHT SPECTRUM

Name _____

Label the colors coming through this prism as the white light is reflected through it.

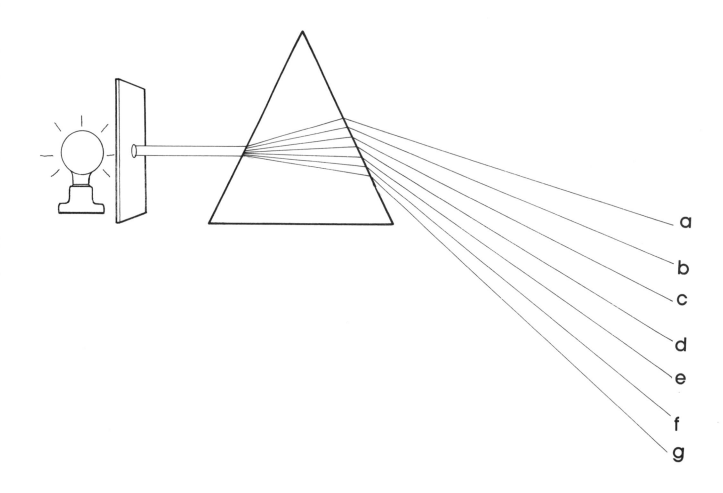

a) _____

b) _____

c) _____

d) _____

e) _____

f) _____

g) _____

LIGHT MATCHING

Match the definition or corresponding phrase in Column II with the correct word in Column I.

I		II
1. hertz	_____	a) the angle at which a ray "bounces off" a surface
2. wave velocity	_____	b) bending of light waves when they pass through another substance
3. frequency	_____	c) an imaginary line drawn at a right angle to the surface of a barrier
4. reflection	_____	d) number of waves that pass a given point in one second
5. wavelength	_____	e) tells how much a ray of light will bend as it travels through a given material
6. refraction	_____	f) translucent material that separates white light into colors
7. crest	_____	g) frequency times wavelength
8. trough	_____	h) lowest part of a wave
9. photon	_____	i) type of electromagnetic radiation
10. light	_____	j) unit for frequency
11. prism	_____	k) the bouncing of a wave off another object
12. index of refraction	_____	l) a continuous band of colors arranged according to wavelength or frequency
13. angle of incidence	_____	m) distance between corresponding points on two waves
14. angle of reflection	_____	n) particle of light
15. visible light spectrum	_____	o) highest point of a wave
16. normal	_____	p) the angle at which a ray of light strikes a surface

MAGNETIC FIELDS

Name _____

Draw the pattern of magnetic fields around these magnets

N   **S**

- -

N   **S**

- -

N   **N**

CALCULATING CURRENT

Name _____

Ohm's Law states that $I = \dfrac{V}{R}$

where I = current (amperes)
         V = voltage (volts)
         R = resistance (ohms)

Solve the following problems.

1. What is the current produced with a 9-volt battery through a resistance of 100 ohms?

   _____

2. Find the current when a 12-volt battery is connected through a resistance of 25 ohms.

   _____

3. If the potential difference is 120 volts and the resistance is 50 ohms, what is the current?

   _____

4. What would be the current in Problem 3 if the potential difference were doubled?

   _____

5. What would be the current in Problem 3 if the resistance were doubled?

   _____

CALCULATING VOLTAGE

Name _____

V	=	I	x	R
Voltage (volts)	=	Current (amperes)	x	Resistance (ohms)

Solve the following problems.

1. What voltage produces a current of 50 amps with a resistance of 20 ohms?

    _____

2. Silver has a resistance of 1.98×10^{-4} ohms. What voltage would produce a current of 100 amps?

    _____

3. A current of 250 amps is flowing through a copper wire with a resistance of 2.09×10^{-4} ohms. What is the voltage?

    _____

4. What voltage produces a current of 500 amps with a resistance of 50 ohms?

    _____

5. What voltage would produce a current of 100 amps through an aluminum wire which has a resistance of 3.44×10^{-4} ohms?

    _____

CALCULATING RESISTANCE

Name _____

$R = \dfrac{V}{I}$	Resistance (ohms) = $\dfrac{\text{Voltage (volts)}}{\text{Current (amperes)}}$

Solve the following problems.

1. What resistance would produce a current of 200 amperes with a potential difference of 2,000 volts?

   _____

2. A 12-volt battery produces a current of 25 amperes. What is the resistance?

   _____

3. A 9-volt battery produces a current of 2.0 amperes. What is the resistance?

   _____

4. An overhead wire has a potential difference of 2,000 volts. If the current flowing through the wire is one million amperes, what is the resistance of the wire?

   _____

5. What is the resistance of a light bulb if a 120-volt potential difference produces a current of 0.8 amperes?

   _____

OHM'S LAW PROBLEMS

Name _____

Using Ohm's Law, solve the following problems.

1. What is the current produced by a potential difference of 240 volts through a resistance of 0.2 ohms?

_____

2. What resistance would produce a current of 120 amps from a 6-volt battery?

_____

3. What voltage is necessary to produce a current of 200 amperes through a resistance of 1×10^{-3} ohms?

_____

4. What is the current produced by a 9-volt battery flowing through a resistance of 2×10^{-4} ohms?

_____

5. What is the potential difference if a resistance of 25 ohms produces a current of 250 amperes?

_____

92 ©Instructional Fair, Inc.

CALCULATING POWER

> P = V x I
> Power (watts) = Voltage (volts) x current (amperes)

Solve the following problems.

1. A 6-volt battery produces a current of 0.5 amps. What is the power in the circuit?

   _____

2. A 100-watt light bulb is operating on 1.2 amperes current. What is the voltage?

   _____

3. A potential difference of 120 volts is operating on a 500-watt microwave oven. What is the current being used?

   _____

4. A light bulb uses 0.625 amperes from a source of 120 volts. How much power is used by the bulb?

   _____

5. What voltage is necessary to run a 500-watt motor with a current of 200 amperes?

   _____

Physical Science IF8767 93 ©Instructional Fair, Inc.

CALCULATING ELECTRICAL ENERGY AND COST

Name _____

One kilowatt hour is 1,000 watts of power for one hour of time. The abbreviation for kilowatt hour is kWh.

> **Example:** A coffee pot operates on 2 amperes of current on a 110-volt circuit for 3 hours. Calculate the total kWh used.
>
> 1. Determine power: $P = V \times I$ $kWh = P \times hours$
>
> $= 110 \text{ volts} \times 2 \text{ amps}$ $kWh = \dfrac{V \times I \times hours}{1,000}$
>
> $= 220 \text{ watts}$
>
> 2. Convert watts to kilowatts:
>
> $220 \text{ watts} \times \dfrac{1 \text{ kilowatt}}{1,000 \text{ watts}} = 0.22 \text{ kW}$
>
> 3. Multiply by the hours given in the problem:
> $0.22 \text{ kW} \times 3 \text{ hrs} = 0.66 \text{ kWh}$

Solve the following problems.

1. A microwave oven operates on 5 amps of current on a 110-volt circuit for one hour. Calculate the total kilowatt hours used. _____

2. How much would it cost to run the microwave in Problem 1 if the cost of energy is $0.10 per kWh? _____

3. An electric stove operates on 20 amps of current on a 220-volt circuit for one hour. Calculate the total kilowatt hours used. _____

4. What is the cost of using the stove in Problem 3 if the cost of energy if $0.10 per kWh? _____

5. A refrigerator operates on 15 amps of current on a 220-volt circuit for 18 hours per day. How many kilowatt hours are used per day? _____

6. If the electric costs are 15¢ per kWh, how much does it cost to run the refrigerator in Problem 5 per day? _____

7. The meter reading on June 1 was 84502 kWh. On July 1, the meter read 87498 kWh. If the cost of electricity in the area was 12¢ per kWh, what was the electric bill for the month of June? _____

8. A room was lighted with three 100-watt bulbs for 5 hours per day. If the cost of electricity was 9¢ per kWh, how much would be saved per day by switching to 60-watt bulbs? _____

SERIES AND PARALLEL CIRCUITS

Name _____

A

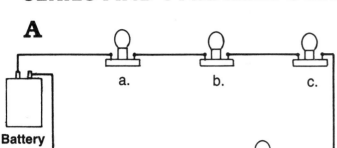

B

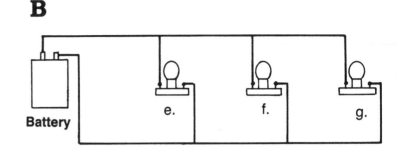

_____   _____

Answer the following questions regarding circuits A and B above.

1. Label circuits A and B as series or parallel.

2. If bulb a burns out, will bulb d still light? _____

3. If bulb f burns out, will bulb g still light? _____

4. If bulbs b, c and d are burned out, will bulb a still light? _____

5. If bulbs f and g are missing, will bulb e still light? _____

6. Draw a diagram of a parallel circuit having 3 light bulbs, 3 switches and a battery. Each light bulb is on a separate switch.

7. Draw a diagram of a series circuit having 3 light bulbs, one switch and a battery.

8. Would series or parallel circuits be better for wiring light in a house? _____

    Why? _____

    _____

AN ELECTRIC MOTOR

Name _____

Label the following parts on the picture of the electric motor below. List the function/ purpose of each part.

horseshoe electromagnet (or permanent magnet) _____

_____

armature _____

_____

commutator _____

_____

brushes (+ and –) _____

_____

field coil _____

_____

current source _____

_____

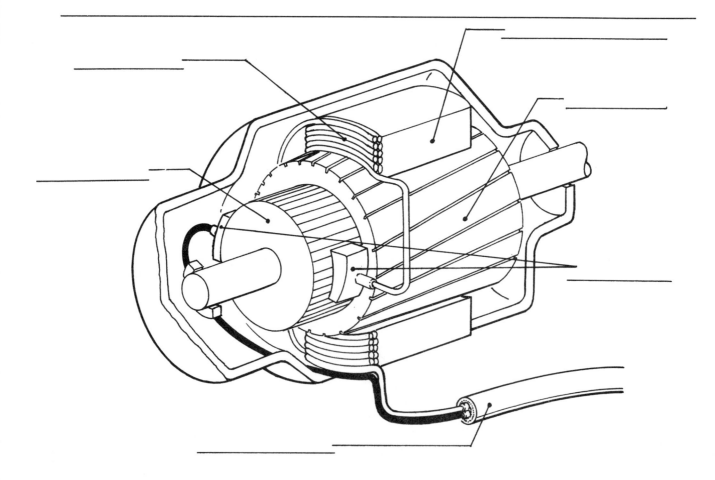

AN ELECTRIC GENERATOR

Name _____

Label the following parts on the picture of the diagrams below of an alternating current and a direct current generator. List the function/purpose of each part.

wire coils _____

_____

brushes _____

_____

slip rings (A.C. only) _____

_____

commutator (D.C. only) _____

_____

armature _____

_____

magnet _____

_____

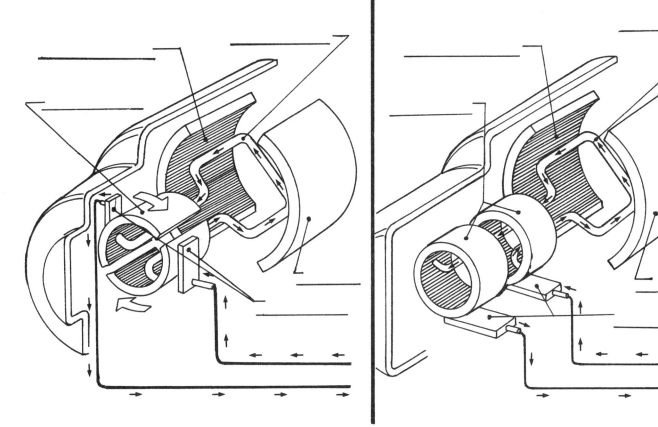

Direct Current

Alternating Current

TRANSFORMERS

Determine the voltage and current in the following transformers.

Step-Up Transformer

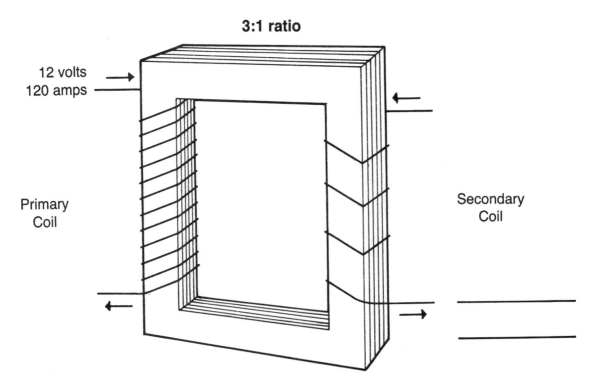

1:2 ratio

6 volts
120 amps

Primary
Coil

Secondary
Coil

Step-Down Transformer

3:1 ratio

12 volts
120 amps

Primary
Coil

Secondary
Coil

98

ELECTRICITY CROSSWORD

Name _____

ACROSS

3. Made from semiconductors and need little voltage
6. An electric _____ converts electrical energy to kinetic energy.
8. Measures current
9. Changes alternating current to direct current
11. This type of circuit may contain thousands of tiny transistors

DOWN

1. Measures potential difference
2. Current that changes direction
4. Magnifies a small electric signal
5. A device that produces current by moving a magnetic field across a wire
7. A semiconductor material
10. A device that uses electrons to produce images on a screen is a _____ ray tube.

HALF-LIFE CALCULATIONS

Name _____

Half-life is the time required for one-half of a radioactive nuclide to decay (change to another element). It is possible to calculate the amount of a radioactive element that will be left if we know its half-life.

Example: The half-life of Po-214 is 0.001 second. How much of a 10 g sample will be left after 0.003 seconds?

Answer: Calculate the number of half-lives:

0.003 seconds x $\dfrac{1 \text{ half-life}}{0.001 \text{ second}}$ = 3 half-lives

After 0 half-lives, 10 g are left.
After 1 half-life, 5 g are left.
After 2 half-lives, 2.5 g are left.
After 3 half-lives, 1.25 g are left.

Solve the following problems.

1. The half-life of radon-222 is 3.8 days. How much of a 100 g sample is left after 15.2 days?

   _____

2. Carbon-14 has a half-life of 5,730 years. If a sample contains 70 mg originally, how much is left after 17,190 years?

   _____

3. How much of a 500 g sample of potassium-42 is left after 62 hours? The half-life of K-42 is 12.4 hours?

   _____

4. The half-life of cobalt-60 is 5.26 years. If 50 g are left after 15.8 years, how many grams were in the original sample?

   _____

5. The half-life of I-131 is 8.07 days. If 25 g are left after 40.35 days, how many grams were in the original sample?

   _____

6. If 100 g of Au-198 decays to 6.25 g in 10.8 days, what is the half-life of Au-198?

   _____

A NUCLEAR REACTOR

Name _____

Label the following parts of a nuclear reactor below. List the function/purpose of each part.

control rods _____

_____

_____

reaction chamber _____

_____

_____

moderator _____

_____

_____

coolant _____

_____

_____

shield _____

_____

_____

turbine generator _____

_____

_____

fuel _____

_____

_____

transformer _____

_____

_____

heat exchanger _____

_____

_____

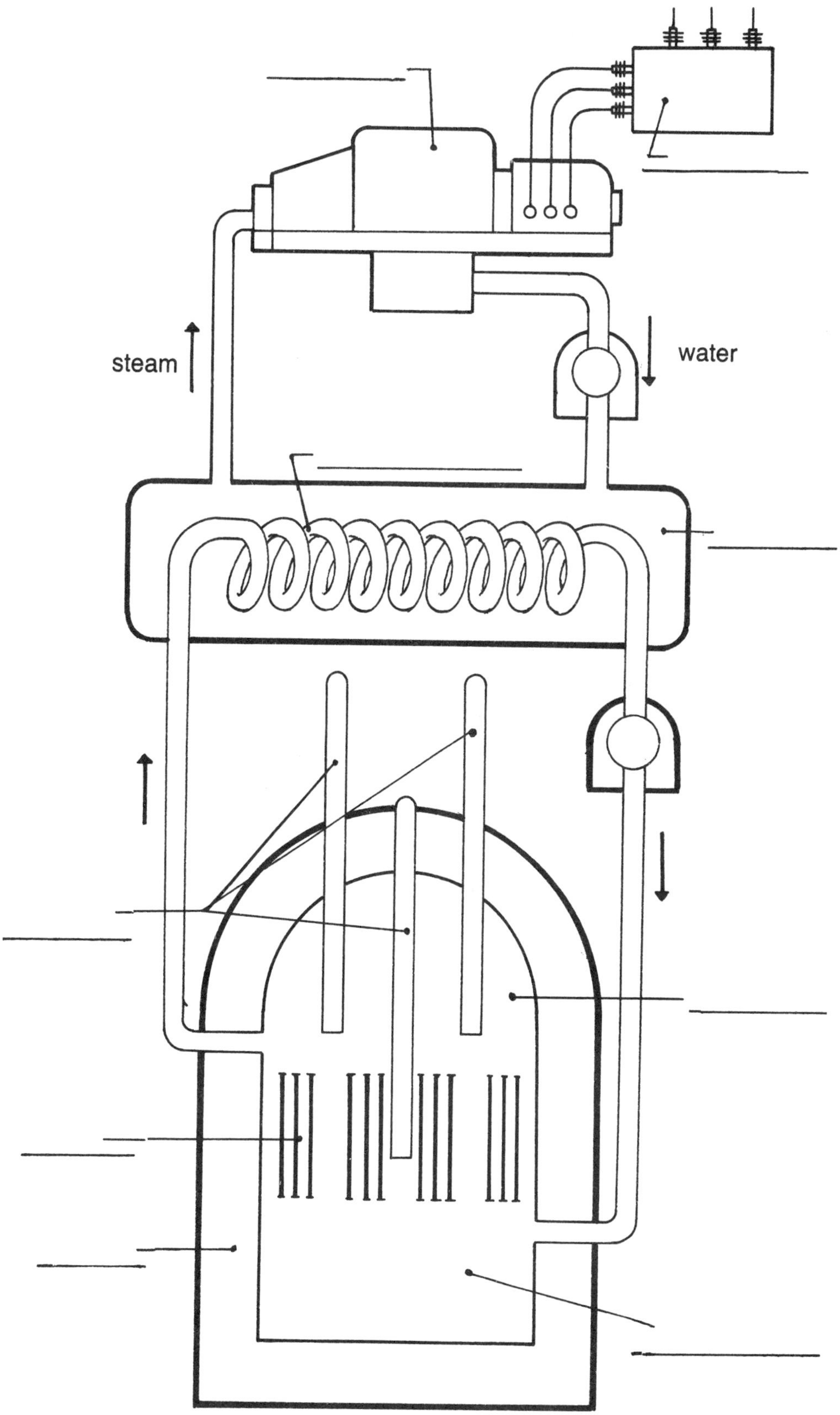

steam

water

FUEL ALTERNATIVES CROSSWORD

Name _____

ACROSS

2. Solar _____ change light energy into electrical energy.
5. Energy that is produced from the splitting of atoms
6. Fuels that are the remains of plants and animals from long ago
8. Fuel for nuclear reactors
9. Power produced from moving water
12. Slows down neutrons

DOWN

1. Uses the kinetic energy of the air to produce power
3. Energy from the sun
4. Heat within the Earth is called _____ energy.
7. Fuels made from materials like plants or coal
10. Absorb neutrons in a nuclear reactor
11. Power produced from the pull of gravity of the moon and sun

ANSWER KEY

SCIENTIFIC METHOD

Name _____

Put the following steps of the scientific method in the proper order.

- **2** Research the problem.
- **5** Observe and record.
- **3** Make a hypothesis.
- **1** Identify the problem.
- **6** Arrive at a conclusion.
- **4** Test the hypothesis.

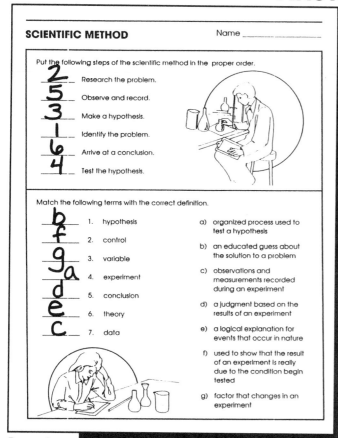

Match the following terms with the correct definition.

- **b** 1. hypothesis
- **f** 2. control
- **g** 3. variable
- **a** 4. experiment
- **d** 5. conclusion
- **e** 6. theory
- **c** 7. data

a) organized process used to test a hypothesis

b) an educated guess about the solution to a problem

c) observations and measurements recorded during an experiment

d) a judgment based on the results of an experiment

e) a logical explanation for events that occur in nature

f) used to show that the result of an experiment is really due to the condition begin tested

g) factor that changes in an experiment

Page 1

SAFETY IN THE LABORATORY

Name _____

What is wrong in the following pictures?

1. no goggles or apron

2. dangling sleeves + no hair pulled back no goggles or apron

3. heating from bottom + perpendicular to desk no goggles or apron

4. too close to burner

5. sniffing directly

6. playing and pushing each other

Page 2

LABORATORY EQUIPMENT

Name _____

Match the following names of lab instruments and equipment with the correct picture.

- a. beaker
- b. graduated cylinder
- c. balance
- d. Bunsen burner
- e. test tube
- f. test tube clamp
- g. funnel
- h. Erlenmeyer flask
- i. tongs
- j. ring stand

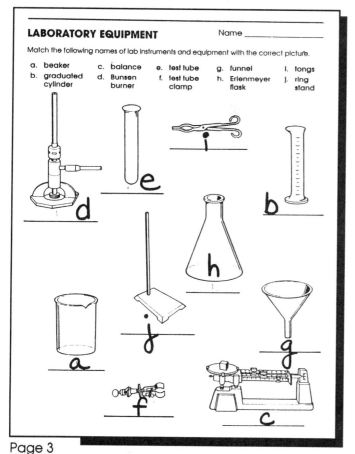

Page 3

USING THE BALANCE

Name _____

The following balance measure mass is grams. What masses are shown on each of the following balances?

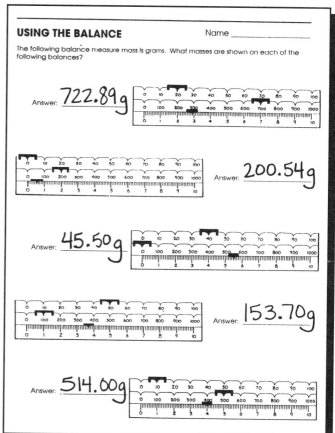

Answer: 722.89g

Answer: 200.54g

Answer: 45.50g

Answer: 153.70g

Answer: 514.00g

Page 4

ANSWER KEY

MEASURING LENGTH

Name _____

What lengths are marked on the following centimeter ruler?

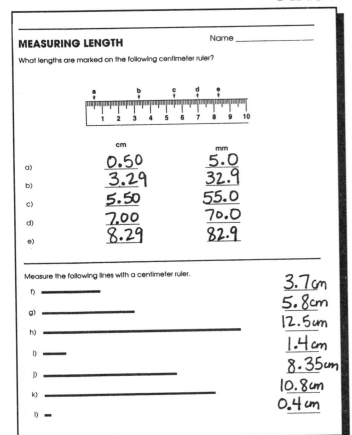

	cm	mm
a)	0.50	5.0
b)	3.29	32.9
c)	5.50	55.0
d)	7.00	70.0
e)	8.29	82.9

Measure the following lines with a centimeter ruler.

f)	3.7 cm
g)	5.8 cm
h)	12.5 cm
i)	1.4 cm
j)	8.35 cm
k)	10.8 cm
l)	0.4 cm

Page 5

MEASURING LIQUIDS

Name _____

What volume is indicated on each of these graduated cylinders? The unit of volume of is mL.

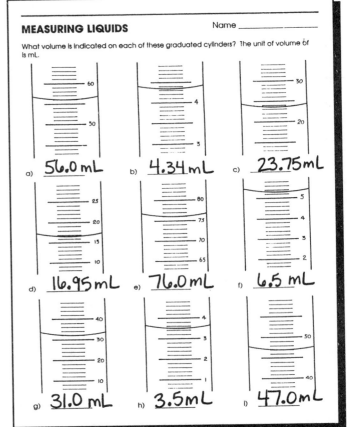

a)	56.0 mL	b)	4.34 mL	c)	23.75 mL
d)	16.95 mL	e)	76.0 mL	f)	6.5 mL
g)	31.0 mL	h)	3.5 mL	i)	47.0 mL

Page 6

READING THERMOMETERS

Name _____

What temperature is indicated on each of these thermometers?

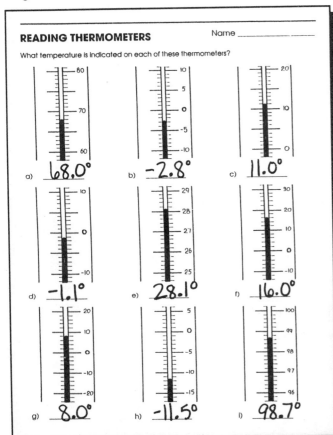

a)	68.0°	b)	-2.8°	c)	11.0°
d)	-1.1°	e)	28.1°	f)	16.0°
g)	8.0°	h)	-11.5°	i)	98.7°

Page 7

METRICS AND MEASUREMENT

Name _____

Scientists use the metric system of measurement, based on the number 10. It is important to be able to convert from one unit to another.

kilo	hecto	deca	**Basic Unit**	deci	centi	milli
(k)	(h)	(da)	gram (g)	(d)	(c)	(m)
1000	100	10	liter (L)	.1	.01	.001
10^3	10^2	10^1	meter (m)	10^{-1}	10^2	10^3

Using the above chart, we can determine how many places to move the decimal point and in what direction by counting the places from one unit to the other.

Example: Convert 5 mL to L.

Answer: To go from milli (m) to the basic unit, liters, count on the above chart three places to the left. Move the decimal point three places to the left and 5 mL becomes 0.005 L.

Convert the following.

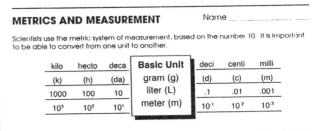

1. 35 mL = 0.35 dL
2. 950 g = 0.950 kg
3. 275 mm = 27.5 cm
4. 1,000 L = 1.000 kL
5. 1,000 mL = 1.000 L
6. 4,500 mg = 4.5 g
7. 25 cm = 250 mm
8. 0.005 kg = 0.5 dag
9. 0.075 m = 7.5 cm
10. 15 g = 15,000 mg

Page 8

ANSWER KEY

UNIT CONVERSIONS AND FACTOR-LABEL METHOD

Name _____

Another method of going from one unit to another involves multiplying by a conversion factor. A conversion factor is a fraction that is equal to the number 1. For example, 60 seconds = 1 hour. Therefore, 60 sec/1 hr or 1 hr/60 sec = 1. When you multiply by the number 1, the value of the number is not changed, although the units may be different.

Example: How many milligrams in 20 kilograms?

Solution: Use the following relationships:

$$1000 \text{ mg} = 1 \text{ g}$$
$$1000 \text{ g} = 1 \text{ kg}$$

1. Start with the original number and unit.
2. Multiply by a unit factor with the unit to be discarded on the bottom and the desired unit on top.
3. Cancel units.
4. Perform numerical calculations.

$$20 \text{ kg} \times \frac{1000 \text{ g}}{1 \text{ kg}} \times \frac{1000 \text{ mg}}{1 \text{ g}} = 20{,}000{,}000 \text{ or } 2 \times 10^7 \text{ mg}$$

Perform the following conversions using unit factoring.

1. 500 mL = **0.5** L
2. 25 cg = **0.25** g
3. 400 mg = **0.0004** kg
4. 30 cm = **300** mm
5. 3500 secs = **0.97** hr
6. 2 yrs = **63,072,000** secs (Assume 1 year = 365 days)
7. 15 m = **15,000** mm
8. 0.75 L = **750** mL
9. 6.4 kg = **6,400** g
10. 7200 m = **7.2** km

11. 4.2 L = **4,200** cm³
12. 0.35 km = **350** m
13. 2.3 L = **2,300** mL
14. 4.5 yds = **162** in
15. 50 mm = **0.00005** km
16. 150 mg = **0.15** g
17. 150 kg = **150,000** g
18. 23 mL = **0.023** L
19. 0.156 g = **156** mg
20. 1.25 L = **1250** mL

Page 9

USING CORRECT UNITS

Name _____

For each of the following commonly used measurements, indicate its symbol. Use the symbols to complete the following.

mL milliliter   **mg** milligram   **L** liter   **cm** centimeter
kg kilogram   **mm** millimeter   **km** kilometer   **g** gram
m meter   **ms** millisecond   **μg** microgram   **nm** nanometer

1. Colas may be purchased in two or three **L** bottles.
2. The mass of bowling ball is 7.25 **kg**.
3. The length of the common housefly is about 1 **cm**.
4. The mass of a paper clip is about 1 **g**.
5. One teaspoon of cough syrup has a volume of 5 **mL**.
6. The speed limit on the highway is usually 106.6 **km**/h or 29 **m**/s.
7. The length of the small intestine in man is about 6.25 **m**.
8. Viruses such as AIDS, polio and flu range in length from 17 to 1000 **nm**.
9. Adults require 1,000 **mg** of calcium to meet the U.S. RDA.
10. In a vacuum, light can travel 300 km in 1 **ms**.
11. The mass of a proton is 1.67×10^{-18} **μg**.
12. Blue light has a wavelength of about 500 **nm**.
13. One mole of oxygen gas at STP occupies 22.4 **L**.
14. Myoglobin, a protein that stores oxygen, has a mass of 2.98×10^{-14} **μg**.
15. Buttery popcorn contained in a large 1 **L** bowl has a mass of about 50 **g** of fat and about 650 calories.
16. The dying comet fragments that continued to batter Jupiter travel at speeds of about 58,117 **mm**/**ms** or 130,000 miles per hour.
17. The human heart has a mass of about 1.05 **kg**.
18. Stand with your arms raised out to your side. The distance from your nose to your outstretched middle finger is about 1 **m**.
19. The body mass of a flea is about 0.5 **mg** and it can jump about 20 **cm** high.
20. On a statistical basis, smoking a single cigarette lowers your life expectancy by 642,000 **ms** or 10.7 minutes.

Page 10

SCIENTIFIC NOTATION

Name _____

Scientists very often deal with very small and very large numbers, which can lead to a lot of confusion when counting zeros! We have learned to express these numbers as powers of 10.

Scientific notation takes the form of $M \times 10^n$ where $1 \le M < 10$ and n represents the number of decimal places to be moved. Positive n indicates the standard form is larger than zero whereas negative n would indicate a number smaller than zero.

Example 1: Convert 1,500,000 to scientific notation.
Move the decimal point so that there is only one digit to its left, a total of 6 places.
$$1{,}500{,}000 = 1.5 \times 10^6$$

Example 2: Convert 0.00025 to scientific notation.
For this, move the decimal point 4 places to the right.
$$0.00025 = 2.5 \times 10^4$$
(Note that when a number starts out less than one, the exponent is always negative.)

Convert the following to scientific notation.

1. 0.005 = **5×10^{-3}**
2. 5,050 = **5.05×10^3**
3. 0.0008 = **8×10^{-4}**
4. 1,000 = **1×10^3**
5. 1,000,000 = **1×10^6**

6. 0.25 = **2.5×10^{-1}**
7. 0.025 = **2.5×10^{-2}**
8. 0.0025 = **2.5×10^{-3}**
9. 500 = **5×10^2**
10. 5,000 = **5×10^3**

Convert the following to standard notation.

1. 1.5×10^3 = **1,500**
2. 1.5×10^3 = **0.0015**
3. 3.75×10^2 = **0.0375**
4. 3.75×10^2 = **375**
5. 2.2×10^5 = **220,000**

6. 3.35×10^1 = **0.335**
7. 1.2×10^4 = **0.00012**
8. 1×10^4 = **10,000**
9. 1×10^1 = **0.1**
10. 4×10^0 = **4**

Page 11

CALCULATIONS USING SIGNIFICANT FIGURES

Name _____

When multiplying numbers in scientific notation, multiply the first part of the number (mantissa) and add exponents.

Example 1: $(3.0 \times 10^2)(2.5 \times 10^6) =$
Answer: Multiply $3.0 \times 2.5 = 7.5$
Add $2 + 6 = 8$
$= 7.5 \times 10^8$

When dividing numbers in scientific notation, divide the first part of the number and subtract exponents.

Example 2: $\dfrac{9.0 \times 10^6}{4.5 \times 10^2}$
Answer: Divide 9.0 by 4.5 = 2.0
Subtract 2 from 6 = 4
$= 2.0 \times 10^4$

Perform the following calculations. Express all answers in scientific notation.

1. $(1.5 \times 10^3)(3.5 \times 10^5)$ **5.3×10^8**	6. $(4 \times 10^5) \div (1 \times 10^{-3})$ **4×10^8**
2. $(2.0 \times 10^8)(2.0 \times 10^6)$ **4.0×10^{14}**	7. $(7.6 \times 10^{-3})(8.2 \times 10^{-4})$ **6.2×10^{-7}**
3. $(6.2 \times 10^6) \div (3.1 \times 10^2)$ **2.0×10^4**	8. $(8.5 \times 10^{-6}) \div (2.5 \times 10^{-1})$ **3.4×10^{-5}**
4. $(5.0 \times 10^4) \div (2.5 \times 10^3)$ **2.0×10^1**	9. $(7.0 \times 10^{11})(7.0 \times 10^{-11})$ **4.9×10^1**
5. $(6.8 \times 10^7)(2.2 \times 10^5)$ **1.5×10^3**	10. $(1.3 \times 10^5) \div (2.6 \times 10^5)$ **5.3×10^3**

Page 12

ANSWER KEY

DENSITY   Name _____

Which has the greater mass, air or lead? Most of you would answer lead, but actually this question does not have an answer. To compare these two things you need to now how much of each you have. A large amount of air could have a greater mass than a small amount of lead. TO compare different things, we have to compare the masses of each that occupy the same space, or volume. This is called density.

$$\text{Density} = \frac{\text{mass}}{\text{volume}}$$

Solve the following problems.

1. What is the density of carbon dioxide gas if 0.196 g occupies a volume of 100 mL?

   1.96×10^{-3} g/mL   Answer: _____

2. A block of wood 3.0 cm on each side has a mass of 27 g. What is the density of this block?

   1.0 g/cm³   Answer: _____

3. An irregularly shaped stone was lowered into a graduated cylinder holding a volume of water equal to 2.0 mL. The height of the water rose to 7.0 mL. If the mass of the stone was 25 g, what was its density?

   5.0 g/mL   Answer: _____

4. A 10.0 cm³ sample of copper has a mass of 89.6 g. What is the density of copper?

   8.96 g/cm³   Answer: _____

5. Silver has a density of 10.5 g/cm³ and gold has a density of 19.3 g/cm³. Which would have a greater mass, 5 cm³ of silver or 5 cm³ of gold?

   gold   Answer: _____

6. Five mL of ethanol has a mass of 3.9 g, and 5.0 mL of benzene has a mass of 4.4 g. Which liquid is denser?

   benzene   Answer: _____

7. A sample of iron has the dimensions of 2 cm x 3 cm x 2 cm. If the mass of this rectangular-shaped object is 94 g, what is the density of iron?

   7.8 g/cm³   Answer: _____

Page 13

GRAPHING OF DATA   Name _____

Graphing is a very important tool in science since it enables us to see trends that are not always obvious. Graph the following data and answer the questions below.

Mass of Liquid (g)	Volume of Liquid (cm³)
20	4
100	20
75	15
40	8
10	2

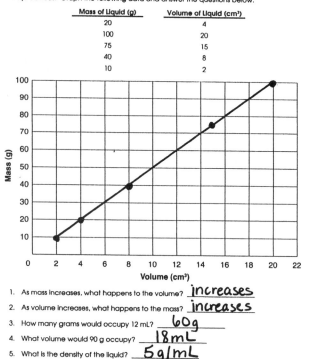

1. As mass increases, what happens to the volume? __increases__

2. As volume increases, what happens to the mass? __increases__

3. How many grams would occupy 12 mL? __60 g__

4. What volume would 90 g occupy? __18 mL__

5. What is the density of the liquid? __5 g/mL__

Page 14

DETERMINING SPEED (VELOCITY)   Name _____

Speed is a measure of how fast an object is moving or traveling. Velocity is a measure of how fast an object is traveling in a certain direction. Both speed and velocity include the distance traveled compared to the amount of time taken to cover this distance.

$$\text{speed} = \frac{\text{distance}}{\text{time}} \qquad \text{velocity} = \frac{\text{distance}}{\text{time}} \text{ in a specific direction}$$

Answer the following questions.

1. What is the velocity of a car that traveled a total of 75 kilometers north in 1.5 hours?

   __50 km/hr__

2. What is the velocity of a planed that traveled 3,000 miles from New York to California in 5.0 hours? __600 mi/hr__

3. John took 45 minutes to bicycle to his grandmother's house, a total of four kilometers. What was his velocity in km/hr? __5.3 km/hr__

4. It took 3.5 hours for a train to travel the distance between two cities at a velocity of 120 km/hr. How many miles lie between the two cities? __420 mi__

5. How long would it take for a car to travel a distance of 200 kilometers if it is traveling at a velocity of 55 km/hr? __3.6 hrs__

6. A car is traveling at 100 km/hr. How many hours will it take to cover a distance of 750 km? __7.5 hrs__

7. A plane traveled for about 2.5 hours at a velocity of 1200 km/hr. What distance did it travel? __3,000 km__

8. A girl is pedaling her bicycle at a velocity of 0.10 km/min. How far will she travel in two hours? __12 km__

9. An ant carries food a at speed on 1 cm/s. How long will it take the ant to carry a cookie crumb from the kitchen table to the ant hill, a distance of 50 m? Express your answer in seconds, minutes and hours. __5000 s, 83.3 min, 1.39 hrs__

10. The water in the Buffalo River flows at an average speed of 5 km/hr. If you and a friend decide to canoe down the river a distance of 16 kilometers, how many hours and minutes will it take? __3 hrs, 12 min__

Page 15

CALCULATING AVERAGE SPEED   Name _____

Graph the following data on the grid below and answer the questions at the bottom of the page.

Time (min)	Distance (m)
0	0
1	50
2	75
3	90
4	110
5	125

$$\text{Average Speed} = \frac{\text{Total Distance}}{\text{Total Time}}$$

1. What is the average speed after two minutes? __37.5 m/min__

2. After three minutes? __30 m/min__

3. After five minutes? __25 m/min__

4. What is the average speed between two and four minutes? __17.5 m/min__

5. What is the average speed between four and five minutes? __15 m/min__

Page 16

ANSWER KEY

ACCELERATION CALCULATIONS

Name _____

Acceleration means a change in speed or direction. It can also be defined as a change in velocity per unit of time.

$$a = \frac{v_f - v_i}{t}$$ where a = velocity
v_f = final velocity
v_i = initial velocity
t = time

Calculate the acceleration for the following data.

	Initial Velocity	Final Velocity	Time	Acceleration
1.	0 km/hr	24 km/hr	3 s	8 km/hr/s
2.	0 m/s	35 m/s	5 s	7 m/s/s
3.	20 km/hr	60 km/hr	10 s	4 m/s/s
4.	50 m/s	150 m/s	5 s	20 m/s/s
5.	25 km/hr	1200 km/hr	2 min	587.5 km/hr/min

6. A car accelerates from a standstill to 60 km/hr in 10.0 seconds.
What is its acceleration?

6 km/hr/s

7. A car accelerates from 25 km/hr to 55 km/hr in 30 seconds.
What is its acceleration?

1 km/hr/s

8. A train is accelerating at a rate of 2.0 km/hr/s.
If its initial velocity is 20 km/hr, what is its velocity after 30 seconds?

80 km/hr

9. A runner achieves a velocity of 11.1 m/s 9 s after he begins.
What is his acceleration?
What distance did he cover?

1.2 m/s/s
100m

Page 17

GRAPHING SPEED VS. TIME

Name _____

Plot the following data on the graph and answer the questions below.

Speed (km/hr)	Time (s)
0.0	0
10.0	2
20.0	4
30.0	6
40.0	8
50.0	10

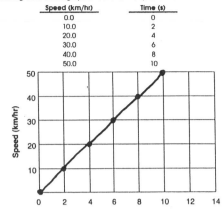

1. As time increases, what happens to the speed? **increases**
2. What is the speed at 5 s? **25 km/hr**
3. Assuming constant acceleration, what would be the speed at 14 s?
70 km/hr
4. At what time would the object reach a speed of 45 km/hr? **9 s**
5. What is the object's acceleration? **5 km/hr/s**
6. What would the shape of the graph be if the speed of 50.0 is maintained from 10 s to 20 s? **horizontal line**
7. Based on the information in Problem 6, calculate the acceleration from 10 s to 20 s.
0 km/hr/s
8. What would the shape of the graph be if the speed of the object decreased from 50.0 km/hr at 20 s to 30 km/hr at 40 s?
9. What is the acceleration in Problem 8? **-1 km/hr/s**

Page 18

GRAPHING DISTANCE VS. TIME

Name _____

Plot the following data on the graph and answer the questions below.

Distance (km)	Time (s)
0	0
5	10
12	20
20	30
30	40
42	50
56	60

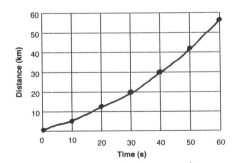

1. What is the average speed at t = 20 s? **0.60 km/s**
2. What is the average speed at t= 30 s? **0.67 km/s**
3. What is the acceleration between 20 s and 30 s? **0.007 km/s/s**
4. What is the average speed at t = 40 s? **0.75 km/s**
5. What is the average speed at t = 60 s? **0.93 km/s**
6. What is the acceleration between 40 s and 60 s? **0.009 km/s/s**
7. Is the object accelerating at a constant rate? **no**

Page 19

GRAVITY AND ACCELERATION (I)

Name _____

The acceleration of a freely falling body is 9.8 m/sec/sec due to the force of gravity.

Using the formula, $a = \frac{v_f - v_i}{t}$, we can calculate the velocity of a falling object at any time if the initial velocity is known.

Example:	What is the velocity of a rubber ball dropped from a building roof after 5 seconds?
Answer:	9.8 m/sec/sec = $\frac{v_f - 0}{5 \text{ sec}}$
	v_f = 49 m/sec

Solve the following problems.

1. What is the velocity of a quarter dropped from a tower after 10 seconds?

98 m/sec   Answer: _____

2. If a block of wood dropped from a tall building has attained a velocity of 78.4 m/s, how long has it been falling?

8 sec   Answer: _____

3. If a ball that is freely falling has attained a velocity of 19.6 m/s after two seconds, what is its velocity five seconds later?

68.6 m/s   Answer: _____

4. A piece of metal has attained a velocity of 107.8 m/sec after falling for 10 seconds. What is its initial velocity?

9.8 m/sec   Answer: _____

5. How long will it take an object that falls from rest to attain a velocity of 147 m/sec?

15 sec   Answer: _____

Page 20

ANSWER KEY

GRAVITY AND ACCELERATION (II)   Name _____

The distance covered by a freely falling body is calculated by the following formula:

$$d = \frac{at^2}{2}$$

where d = distance
a = acceleration
t = time

Example 1: How far will an object fall in 5 seconds?
Answer: $s = \frac{9.8 \text{ m/s}^2 \,(5s)^2}{2} = 122.5$ meters

Example 2: What is the average velocity of a ball that attains a velocity of 39.2 m/s after 4 seconds?
Answer: $va = \frac{v_f - v_i}{2} = \frac{39.2 - 0}{2} = 19.6$ m/s

Solve the following problems.

1. How far will a rubber ball fall in 10 seconds?
490 m   Answer: _____

2. How far will a rubber ball fall in 20 seconds?
1,960 m   Answer: _____

3. How long will it take an object dropped from a window to fall a distance of 78.4 meters?
4 sec   Answer: _____

4. Calculate the final velocity of the ball in Problem 1.
98 m/s   Answer: _____

5. What is the average velocity of the ball in Problem 1?
49 m/s   Answer: _____

6. An airplane is traveling at an altitude of 31,360 meters. A box of supplies is dropped from its cargo hold. How long will it take to reach the ground?
80 sec   Answer: _____

7. At what velocity will the box in Problem 6 be traveling when it hits the ground?
784 m/s   Answer: _____

8. What is the average velocity of the box in Problem 6?
392 m/s   Answer: _____

Page 21

FORCE DIAGRAMS   Name _____

Find the resultant force in each of the following diagrams and draw the resultant vector. Use a ruler and a protractor where necessary. Scale: 1 cm = 10 N, where N represents Newtons of force.

1.   20 N ←→ 30 N   **10 N →**

2.   ← 20 N   ← 30 N   **← 50 N**

3.   30 N   **42 N**   30 N

4.   30 N   **55 N**   45°   30 N

5.   30 N   **30 N**   12 N 135°   30 N

6.   30 N **40 N**   15 N 45° 157.5°   30 N

Page 22

FORCE AND ACCELERATION   Name _____

A force is a push or a pull. To calculate force, we use the following formula,

$$F = ma$$ where F = force in Newtons
m = mass in kg
a = acceleration in m/sec²

Example: With what force will a rubber ball hit the ground if it has a mass of 0.25 kg?
Answer: F = (0.25 kg) (9.8 m/s²)
F = 2.45 N

Solve the following problems.

1. With what force will a car hit a tree if the car has a mass of 3,000 kg and it is accelerating at a rate of 2 m/s²?
6,000 N   Answer: _____

2. A 10 kg bowling ball would require what force to accelerate it down an alleyway at a rate of 3 m/s²?
30 N   Answer: _____

3. What is the mass of a falling rock if it hits the ground with a force of 147 Newtons?
15 kg   Answer: _____

4. What is the acceleration of a softball if it has a mass of 0.50 kg and hits the catcher's glove with a force of 25 Newtons?
50 m/s²   Answer: _____

5. What is the mass of a truck if it is accelerating at a rate of 5 m/s² and hits a parked car with a force of 14,000 Newtons?
2,800 kg   Answer: _____

Page 23

MOTION MATCHING   Name _____

Match the correct term in Column I with is definition in Column II.

I		II
1. **g** kinetic		a) amount of matter in an object
2. **j** centripetal		b) amount of force exerted on an object due to gravity
3. **a** mass		c) distance covered per unit of time
4. **d** acceleration		d) rate at which velocity changes over time
5. **e** velocity		e) speed in a given direction
6. **b** weight		f) unit of measurement for force
7. **k** gravity		g) energy of motion
8. **h** inertia		h) tendency of a moving object to keep moving
9. **c** speed		i) depends on the mass and velocity of an object
10. **i** momentum		j) type of force that keeps objects moving in a circle
11. **f** Newton		k) attractive force between two objects

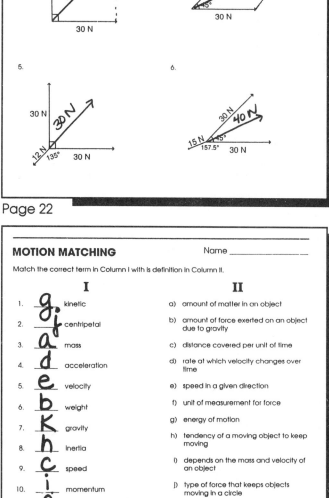

Page 24

ANSWER KEY

HEAT CALCULATIONS

Name _____

Heat is measured in units of joules or calories. The amount of heat given off or absorbed can be calculated by the following formula.

> Q = m x ΔT x C
> heat = (mass in grams) (temperature change) (specific heat)
> The specific heat of water = 1.0 cal/g C° or 4.2 joules/g C°

Solve the following problems.

1. How many calories are absorbed by a pot of water with a mass of 500 g in order to raise the temperature from 20° C to 30° C?

   5,000 cal

   Answer: _____

2. How many joules would be absorbed for the water in Problem 1?

   21,000 joules

   Answer: _____

3. If the specific heat of iron = 0.46 J/g C°, how much heat is needed to warm 50 g of iron from 20° C to 100° C?

   1,840 joules

   Answer: _____

4. If it takes 105 calories to warm 100 g of aluminum from 20° C to 25° C, what is the specific heat of aluminum?

   0.21 cal/g C°

   Answer: _____

5. If it takes 31,500 joules of heat to warm 750 g of water, what was the temperature change?

   10° C

   Answer: _____

Page 25

HEAT AND PHASE CHANGES

Name _____

During a phase change, the temperature remains the same. For these calculations, we use the following formulas.

> For freezing and melting,   heat = (mass in grams) (heat of fusion)
> For boiling and condensation, heat = (mass in grams) (heat of vaporization)
> The heat of fusion of water = 340 J/g
> The heat of vaporization of water = 2,300 J/g

Solve the following problems.

1. How many joules of heat are necessary to melt 500 g or ice at its freezing point?

   170,000 J or 1.7 x 10⁵ J

   Answer: _____

2. How many kilojoules is this?

   170 kilojoules

   Answer: _____

3. How much heat is necessary to vaporize 500 g of water at its boiling point?

   1,150,000 J or 1.15 x 10⁶ J

   Answer: _____

4. If 5,100 joules of heat are given off when a sample of water freezes, what is the mass of the water?

   15g

   Answer: _____

5. If 57,500 joules of heat are given off when a sample of steam condenses, what is the mass of the steam?

   25g

   Answer: _____

Page 26

SIMPLE MACHINES

Name _____

What types of simple machines are shown in the following pictures?

 pulley

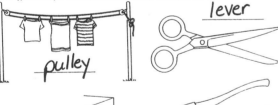 **lever**

inclined plane

wedge

wheel + axle

lever

inclined plane

 **lever**

screw

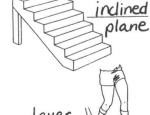 **wheel + axle**

Page 27

TYPES OF LEVERS

Name _____

Classify the following levers as first, second or third class.

 **first class**

 **second class**

 **third class**

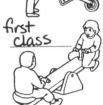 **first class**

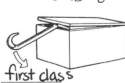 **first class**

 third class

 second class

    **second class**

Page 28

ANSWER KEY

POTENTIAL AND KINETIC ENERGY   Name _____

Potential energy is stored energy due to position. Kinetic energy is energy that depends on mass and velocity (movement).

> Potential Energy = Weight x Height (P.E. = w x h)
> Kinetic Energy = ½ Mass x Velocity² (K.E. = ½mv²)
> The units used are: Energy = joules
>   Weight = newtons
>   Height = meters
>   Mass = kilograms
>   Velocity = m/s

For a closed system, the sum of the potential energy and the kinetic energy is a constant. As the potential energy decreases, the kinetic energy increases.

Solve the following problems.

1. What is the potential energy of a rock that weighs 100 newtons that is sitting on top of a hill 300 meters high?
   30,000 joules   Answer: _____

2. What is the kinetic energy of a bicycle with a mass of 14 kg traveling at a velocity of 3 m/s?
   63 joules   Answer: _____

3. A flower pot weighing 3 newtons is sitting on a windowsill 30 meters from the ground. Is the energy of the flower pot potential or kinetic? How many joules is this?
   potential, 90 joules Answers: _____

4. When the flower pot in Problem 3 is only 10 meters from the ground, what is its potential energy?
   30 joules   Answer: _____

5. How much of the total energy in Problems 3 and 4 has been transformed to kinetic energy?
   60 joules   Answer: _____

6. A 1200 kg automobile is traveling at a velocity of 100 m/s. Is its energy potential or kinetic? How much energy does it possess?
   Kinetic, 6×10^6 joules Answers: _____

Page 29

CALCULATING WORK   Name _____

Work has a special meaning in science. It is the product of the force applied to an object and the distance the object moves. The unit of work is the joule (J).

> W = Force x Distance
> W = F x d   Force = newtons
>   Distance = meters

Solve the following problems.

1. A book weighing 1.0 newton is lifted 2 meters. How much work was done?
   2 joules   Answer: _____

2. A force of 15 newtons is used to push a box along the floor a distance of 3 meters. How much work was done?
   45 joules   Answer: _____

3. It took 50 joules to push a chair 5 meters across the floor. With what force was the chair pushed?
   10 newtons   Answer: _____

4. A force of 100 newtons was necessary to lift a rock. A total of 150 joules of work was done. How far was the rock lifted??
   1.5 meters   Answer: _____

5. It took 500 newtons of force to push a car 4 meters. How much work was done?
   2,000 joules   Answer: _____

6. A young man exerted a force of 9,000 newtons on a stalled car but was unable to move it. How much work was done?
   0 joules   Answer: _____

Page 30

MECHANICAL ADVANTAGE   Name _____

What is the mechanical advantage of the following simple machines?

$$MA = \frac{F_R}{F_E} \quad \text{where } F_R = \text{resistance force}$$
$$F_E = \text{effort force}$$

1.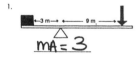
   MA = 3

2.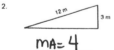
   MA = 4

3.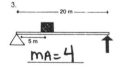
   MA = 4

4.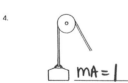
   MA = 1

5.
   MA = 5

6.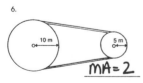
   MA = 2

7.
   MA = 2

8.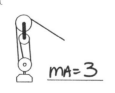
   MA = 3

Page 31

CALCULATING EFFICIENCY   Name _____

The amount of work obtained from a machine is always less than the amount of work put into it. This is because some of the work is lost due to friction. The efficiency of a machine can be calculated using the following formula.

$$\text{percent efficiency} = \frac{\text{work output} \times 100}{\text{work input}}$$

What is the efficiency of the following machines?

1. A man expends 100 J of work to move a box up an inclined plane. The amount of work produced is 80 J.
   80%   Answer: _____

2. A box weighing 100 newtons is pushed up an inclined plane that is 5 meters long. It takes a force of 75 newtons to push it to the top, which has a height of 3 meters.
   45%   Answer: _____

3. Using a lever, a person applies 60 newtons of force and moves the lever 1 meter. This moves a 200 newton rock at the other end by 0.2 meters.
   67%   Answer: _____

4. A person in a wheelchair exerts a force of 25 newtons to go up a ramp that is 10 meters long. The weight of the person and wheelchair is 60 newtons and the height of the ramp is 3 meters.
   72%   Answer: _____

5. A boy pushes a lever down 2 meters with a force of 75 newtons. The box at the other end with a weight of 50 newtons moves up 2.5 meters.
   83%   Answer: _____

6. A pulley system operates with 40% efficiency. If the work put in is 200 joules, how much useful work is produced?
   80 J   Answer: _____

Page 32

ANSWER KEY

CALCULATING POWER

Name _____

Power is the amount of work done per unit of time. The unit for power, joules/second, is the watt.

$$Power = \frac{work}{time}$$
work = joules
time = seconds

Solve the following problems.

1. A set of pulleys is used to lift a piano weighing 1,000 newtons. The piano is lifted 3 meters in 60 seconds. How much power is used?

   50 watts

   Answer: _____

2. How much power is used if a force of 35 newtons is used to push a box a distance of 10 meters in 5 seconds?

   70 watts

   Answer: _____

3. What is the power of a kitchen blender if it can perform 3,750 joules of work in 15 seconds?

   250 watts

   Answer: _____

4. How much work is done using a 500-watt microwave oven for 5 minutes?

   150,000 joules

   Answer: _____

5. How much work is done using a using a 60-watt light bulb for 1 hour?

   216,000 joules

   Answer: _____

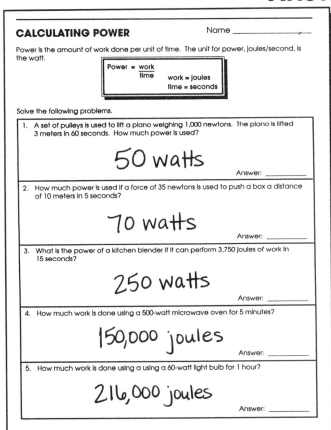

Page 33

FORCE AND WORK CROSSWORD

Name _____

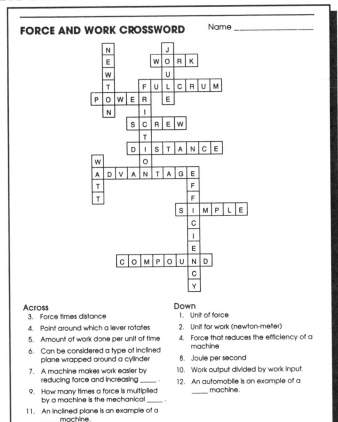

Across
3. Force times distance
4. Point around which a lever rotates
5. Amount of work done per unit of time
6. Can be considered a type of inclined plane wrapped around a cylinder
7. A machine makes work easier by reducing force and increasing ____ .
9. How many times a force is multiplied by a machine is the mechanical ____ .
11. An inclined plane is an example of a ____ machine.

Down
1. Unit of force
2. Unit for work (newton-meter)
4. Force that reduces the efficiency of a machine
8. Joule per second
10. Work output divided by work input.
12. An automobile is an example of a ____ machine.

Page 34

SUBSTANCES VS. MIXTURES

Name _____

A substance is matter for which a chemical formula can be written. Elements and compounds are substances. Mixtures can be in any proportion, and the parts are not chemically bonded.

Classify the following as to whether it is a substance or a mixture by writing S or M in the space provided.

1. sodium — **S**
2. water — **S**
3. soil — **M**
4. coffee — **M**
5. oxygen — **S**
6. alcohol — **S**
7. carbon dioxide — **S**
8. cake batter — **M**
9. air — **M**
10. soup — **M**

11. iron — **S**
12. salt water — **M**
13. ice cream — **M**
14. nitrogen — **S**
15. eggs — **M**
16. blood — **M**
17. table salt — **S**
18. nail polish — **M**
19. milk — **M**
20. cola — **M**

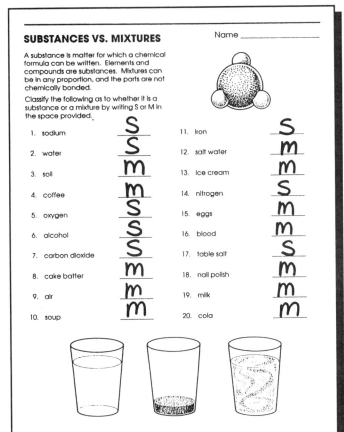

Page 35

HOMOGENEOUS VS. HETEROGENEOUS MATTER

Name _____

Classify the following substances and mixtures as either homogeneous or heterogeneous. Place a √ in the correct column.

	HOMOGENEOUS	HETEROGENEOUS
1. flat soda pop	√	
2. cherry vanilla ice cream		√
3. salad dressing		√
4. sugar	√	
5. soil		√
6. aluminum foil	√	
7. black coffee	√	
8. sugar water	√	
9. city air		√
10. paint		√
11. alcohol	√	
12. iron	√	
13. beach sand		√
14. pure air	√	
15. spaghetti sauce		√

Page 36

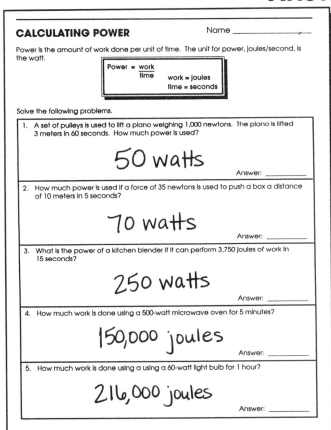

ANSWER KEY

SOLUTIONS, COLLOIDS AND SUSPENSIONS

Name _____

Label the following mixtures as a solution, colloid or suspension. Give an example of each.

Answers will vary.

1. large particles, settles out on standing

Kind of mixture: Suspension

Example: Chocolate milk, muddy H₂O, Orange juice, oil + vinegar salad dressing

2. medium size particles, settles out on standing scatters light

Kind of mixture: Colloid

Example: fog, smoke, whipped cream, milk, marshmallow

3. very small particles does not settle out on standing

Kind of mixture: Solution

Example: salt water, sugar water, 3% hydrogen peroxide

PHYSICAL VS. CHEMICAL PROPERTIES

Name _____

A physical property is observed with the senses and can be determined without destroying the object. For example, color, shape, mass, length, density, specific heat and odor are all examples of physical properties.

A chemical property indicates how a substance reacts with something else. When a chemical property is observed, the original substance is changed into a different substance. For example, the ability of iron to rust is a chemical property. The iron has reacted with oxygen and the original iron metal is gone. It is now iron oxide, a new substance. All chemical changes include physical changes.

Classify the following properties as either chemical or physical by putting a check in the appropriate column.

		Physical Property	Chemical Property
1.	red color	✓	
2.	density	✓	
3.	flammability		✓
4.	solubility	✓	
5.	reacts with acid to form hydrogen		✓
6.	supports combustion		✓
7.	bitter taste	✓	
8.	melting point	✓	
9.	reacts with water to form a gas		✓
10.	reacts with a base to form water		✓
11.	hardness	✓	
12.	boiling point	✓	
143.	can neutralize a base		✓
14.	luster	✓	
15.	odor	✓	

PHYSICAL VS. CHEMICAL CHANGE

Name _____

In a physical change, the original substance still exists. It has only changed in form. Energy changes usually do not accompany physical changes, except in phase changes and when substances dissolve.

In a chemical change, a new substance is produced. Energy changes always accompany chemical changes. Chemical changes are always accompanied by physical changes.

Classify the following as examples of a physical change, a chemical change or both kinds of change.

1. Sodium hydroxide dissolves in water.   physical

2. Hydrochloric acid reacts with sodium hydroxide to produce a salt, water and heat.   chemical

3. A pellet of sodium is sliced in two.   physical

4. Water is heated and changed to steam.   physical

5. Potassium chlorate decomposes to potassium chloride and oxygen gas.   chemical

6. Iron rusts.   chemical

7. Ice melts.   physical

8. Acid on limestone produces carbon dioxide gas.   chemical

9. Milk sours.   chemical

10. Wood rots.   chemical

SEPARATION OF MIXTURES

Name _____

Taking advantage of various physical and chemical properties, how would you separate the following mixtures into their components?

1. Sand and water   filter out the sand, or evaporate off the water

2. Sugar and water   evaporate off the water

3. Oil and water   allow them to separate due to different densities, then skim off the oil on top

4. Sand and gravel   use a sieve to strain out the particles of larger size

5. A mixture of heptane (boiling point 98°C) and heptanol (boiling point 176°C)   Heat to 98°C, allowing heptane to boil off. This can be contained and condensed. The heptanol will remain in liquid form.

6. A mixture of iodine solid and sodium chloride (Hint: Iodine not soluble in water.)   Mix with water. The sodium chloride will dissolve and the iodine will not. Filter out the iodine. The sodium chloride can then be recovered by evaporation.

7. A mixture of lead and aluminum pellets   separate them by hand based on their appearance or shake them in water and allow them to settle in different layers due to different densities

8. A mixture of salt and iron filings   The iron filings can be separated out by a magnet.

©Instructional Fair, Inc.

ANSWER KEY

STATES OF MATTER CROSSWORD

Name _____

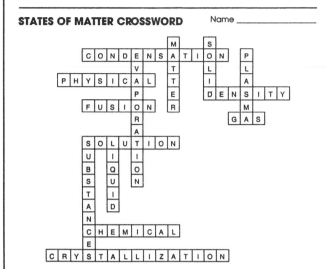

ACROSS

3. Change of a gas to a liquid
6. This type of property can be observed without destroying the substance.
7. Mass of a substance divided by unit volume
8. Physical change of a liquid to a solid at the melting point
9. State of matter having no definite volume or shape
10. Homogeneous mixture
12. This type of change produces a new substance.
13. Change of a liquid to a solid

DOWN

1. Anything that has mass and takes up space
2. State in which atoms or molecules are very close together and are regularly arranged
4. Change of a liquid to a gas
5. This state of matter consists of electrically charged particles.
10. Elements and compounds
11. State of matter having a definite volume but no definite shape.

Page 41

ELEMENTS AND THEIR SYMBOLS

Name _____

Write the symbols for the following elements.

1. oxygen — O
2. hydrogen — H
3. chlorine — Cl
4. sodium — Na
5. fluorine — F
6. carbon — C
7. helium — He
8. nitrogen — N
9. copper — Cu
10. sulfur — S
11. magnesium — Mg
12. manganese — Mn
13. neon — Ne
14. bromine — Br
15. phosphorus — P
16. silver — Ag
17. lead — Pb
18. iron — Fe
19. calcium — Ca
20. potassium — K

Write the name of the element that corresponds to each of the following symbols.

21. Cu — copper
22. K — potassium
23. C — carbon
24. Au — gold
25. Zn — zinc
26. Pb — lead
27. Fe — iron
28. Na — sodium
29. S — sulfur
30. Al — aluminum
31. Ca — calcium
32. Ag — silver
33. P — phosphorus
34. O — oxygen
35. I — iodine
36. Sn — tin
37. H — hydrogen
38. F — fluorine
39. Ni — nickel
40. Hg — mercury

Page 42

ELEMENTS CROSSWORD

Name _____

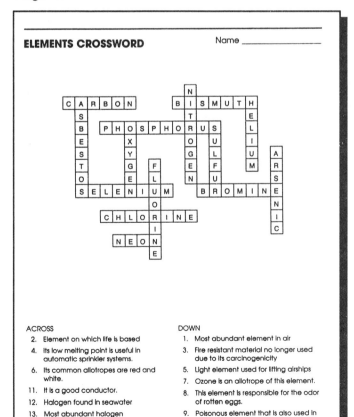

ACROSS

2. Element on which life is based
4. Its low melting point is useful in automatic sprinkler systems.
6. Its common allotropes are red and white.
11. It is a good conductor.
12. Halogen found in seawater
13. Most abundant halogen
14. Gas used in lighted signs to produce a red color

DOWN

1. Most abundant element in air
3. Fire resistant material no longer used due to its carcinogenicity
5. Light element used for lifting airships
7. Ozone is an allotrope of this element.
8. This element is responsible for the odor of rotten eggs.
9. Poisonous element that is also used in medicines and rat poison
10. Most reactive nonmetal

Page 43

PARTS OF AN ATOM

Name _____

An atom is made up of protons and neutrons which are in the nucleus, and electrons which are in the electron cloud surrounding the atom.

The atomic number equals the number of protons. The electrons in a neutral atom equal the number of protons. The mass number equals the sum of the protons and neutrons.

The charge indicates the number of electrons that have been lost or gained. A positive charge indicates the number of electrons (which are negatively charged) lost. A negative charge indicates the number of electrons gained.

This structure can be written as part of a chemical symbol.

> **Example:**
> mass number ↓ charge
> $^{12}_{6}C^{+4}$
> atomic number
> This carbon ion would have 6 protons, 6 neutrons and 2 electrons.

Complete the following chart.

Element/Ion	Atomic Number	Mass Number	Charge	Protons	Neutrons	Electrons
$^{24}_{12}Mg$	12	24	0	12	12	12
$^{39}_{19}K$	19	39	0	19	20	19
$^{23}_{11}Na^{+1}$	11	23	+1	11	12	10
$^{19}_{9}F^{-1}$	9	19	-1	9	10	10
$^{27}_{13}Al^{+3}$	13	27	+3	13	14	10
$^{1}_{1}H$	1	1	0	1	0	1
$^{24}Mg^{2+}$	12	24	+2	12	12	10
Ag	47	108	0	47	61	47
S^{-2}	16	32	-2	16	16	18
$^{2}_{1}H$	1	2	0	1	1	1
$^{35}Cl^{-}$	17	35	-1	17	18	18
Be^{2+}	4	9	+2	4	5	2

Page 44

BOHR MODELS

Name _____

Draw Bohr models of the following atoms.

1. ^1_1H

(2P) 1e-

2. ^4_2He

(2P 2N) 2e-

3. ^7_3Li

(3P 4N) 2e- 1e-

4. $^{23}_{11}Na$

(11P 12N) 1e- 8e- 2e-

5. $^{35}_{17}Cl$

(17P 18N) 8e- 2e- 7e-

6. $^{64}_{29}Cu$

(29P 35N) 1e- 18e- 2e- 8e-

Page 45

PROPERTIES OF METALS AND NONMETALS

Name _____

For the following physical and chemical properties, put a check in the appropriate column if it applies to a metal or a nonmetal.

Property	Metal	Nonmetal
1. malleable	✓	
2. lustrous	✓	
3. gaseous at room temperature		✓
4. forms negative ions		✓
5. metallic bonding	✓	
6. more than 4 valence electrons		✓
7. conducts electricity in solid state	✓	
8. ductile	✓	
9. brittle		✓
10. only forms positive ions	✓	
11. nonconductor		✓
12. covalent bonding		✓
13. can have both positive and negative oxidation numbers		✓
14. gives away electrons in chemical reactions	✓	
15. prefers to receive electrons in chemical reactions		✓

Page 46

ACTIVITY OF THE ELEMENTS

Name _____

Since metals prefer to give away electrons during chemical bonding, the most active metals are closest to Francium, which is a large atom with low ionization energy and electronegativity. Nonmetals prefer to pull in electrons, so the most active nonmetals are closest to fluorine, which has a high ionization energy and electronegativity. The noble gases (Group 18) are considered inactive since they already have a stable octet of electrons in their outer shell.

Referring to a periodic table, circle the member of each pair of elements which is most chemically active.

1. Li and (Na)
2. Cl_2 and (F_2)
3. (N_2) and Ne
4. (Rb) and Ca
5. Ti and (Ca)
6. (K) and Mg
7. (O_2) and S
8. I_2 and (Br_2)
9. (Na) and Zn
10. P and (S)
11. N_2 and (O_2)
12. (Cl_2) and Ar
13. Ba and (Fr)
14. (Rb) and Cu
15. (Be) and Cr

16. (Cl_2) and Br_2
17. Xe and (I_2)
18. Fe and (Ra)
19. (Sr) and Mn
20. (K) and Na
21. Au and (Mg)
22. (S) and Rn
23. (Li) and Be
24. Se and (Br_2)
25. I_2 and (F_2)
26. (Rb) and Sr
27. Ba and (Ra)
28. (Na) and Mg
29. Te and (I_2)
30. (Ca) and Rn

Page 47

PERIODIC TABLE PUZZLE

Name _____

Group Number

1 2 3 4 5 6 7 8 9 10 11 12 13 14 15 16 17 18

I

F G H

B A

C E J

D

Place the letter of each of the above elements next to its description below. Each answer may be used only once, so choose the best answer in each case.

1. An alkali metal **C**
2. An alkali earth metal **F**
3. An inactive gas **A**
4. An active nonmetal **H**
5. A semimetal **B**
6. An inner transition element **D**
7. Its most common oxidation state is -2. **G**
8. A metal with more than one oxidation state **E**
9. Metal with an oxidation number of +3 **J**
10. Has oxidation numbers of +1 and -1 **I**

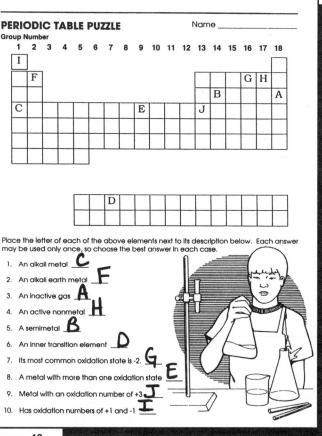

Page 48

ANSWER KEY

PERIODIC TABLE CROSSWORD

Name _____

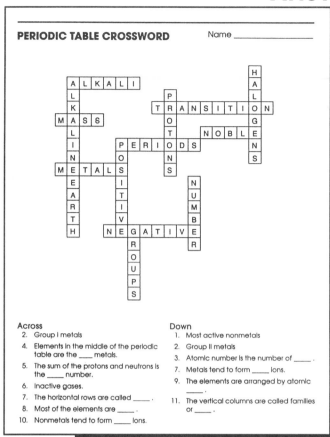

Across
2. Group I metals
4. Elements in the middle of the periodic table are the ___ metals.
5. The sum of the protons and neutrons is the ___ number.
6. Inactive gases.
7. The horizontal rows are called ___ .
8. Most of the elements are ___ .
10. Nonmetals tend to form ___ ions.

Down
1. Most active nonmetals
2. Group II metals
3. Atomic number is the number of ___ .
7. Metals tend to form ___ ions.
9. The elements are arranged by atomic ___ .
11. The vertical columns are called families or ___ .

Page 49

TYPES OF CHEMICAL BONDS

Name _____

Classify the following compounds as ionic (metal and nonmetal), covalent (nonmetal and nonmetal) or both (compound containing a polyatomic ion).

1. $CaCl_2$ — ionic
2. CO_2 — covalent
3. H_2O — covalent
4. $BaSO_4$ — both
5. K_2O — ionic
6. NaF — ionic
7. Na_2CO_3 — both
8. CH_4 — covalent
9. SO_3 — covalent
10. LiBr — ionic

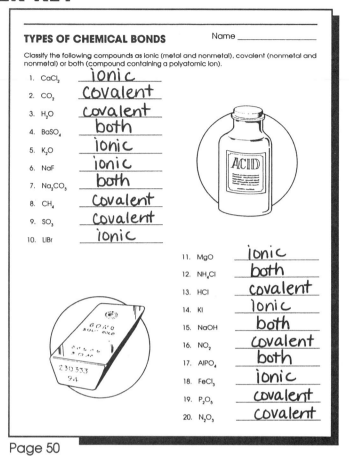

11. MgO — ionic
12. NH_4Cl — both
13. HCl — covalent
14. KI — ionic
15. NaOH — both
16. NO_2 — covalent
17. $AlPO_4$ — both
18. $FeCl_3$ — ionic
19. P_2O_5 — covalent
20. N_2O_3 — covalent

Page 50

NUMBER OF ATOMS IN A FORMULA

Name _____

Determine the number of atoms in the following chemical formulas.

1. NaCl — 2
2. H_2SO_4 — 7
3. KNO_3 — 5
4. $CrCl_2$ — 3
5. C_2H_6 — 8
6. $Ba(OH)_2$ — 5
7. NH_4Br — 6
8. $Ca_3(PO_4)_2$ — 13
9. $Al_2(SO_4)_3$ — 17
10. $Mg(NO_3)_2$ — 9

11. $Cu(NO_3)_2$ — 9
12. $KMnO_4$ — 6
13. H_2O_2 — 4
14. H_3PO_4 — 8
15. $(NH_4)_3PO_4$ — 20
16. Fe_2O_3 — 5
17. $NaC_2H_3O_2$ — 8
18. $Mg(C_2H_3O_2)_2$ — 15
19. Hg_2Cl_2 — 4
20. K_2SO_3 — 6

Page 51

GRAM FORMULA MASS

Name _____

Determine the gram formula mass of each of the following compounds.

1. NaCl — 58g
2. H_2SO_4 — 98g
3. KNO_3 — 101g
4. $CaCl_2$ — 110g
5. C_2H_6 — 30g
6. Ba(OH)2 — 171g
7. NH_4Br — 98g
8. $Ca_3(PO_4)_4$ — 310g
9. $Al_2(SO_4)_3$ — 342g
10. $Mg(NO_3)_2$ — 148g

11. $Cu(NO_3)_2$ — 188g
12. $KMnO_4$ — 158g
13. H_2O_2 — 34g
14. H_3PO_4 — 98g
15. $(NH_4)_3PO_4$ — 149g
16. Fe_2O_3 — 160g
17. $NaC_2H_3O_2$ — 82g
18. $Mg(C_2H_3O_2)_2$ — 142g
19. Hg_2Cl_2 — 472g
20. K_2SO_3 — 158g

Page 52

ANSWER KEY

PERCENTAGE COMPOSITION

Name _____

Solve the following problems.

1. What is the percentage of carbon in CO_2?

27% Answer: _____

2. How many grams of carbon are in 25 g of CO_2?

$6.8g$ Answer: _____

3. What is the percentage of sodium in NaCl?

40% Answer: _____

4. How many grams of sodium are in 75 g of NaCl?

$30g$ Answer: _____

5. What is the percentage of oxygen in $KClO_3$?

39% Answer: _____

6. How many grams of oxygen can be obtained from 5.00 g of $KClO_3$?

$1.95g$ Answer: _____

7. What is the percentage of silver in $AgNO_3$?

64% Answer: _____

8. How many grams of silver can be recovered from 125 g of $AgNO_3$?

$80g$ Answer: _____

9. What is the percentage of gold in $AuCl_3$?

65% Answer: _____

10. How many grams of gold can be recovered from 35.0 g of $AuCl_3$?

$22.8g$ Answer: _____

Page 53

WRITING BINARY FORMULAS

Name _____

Write the formulas for the compounds formed from the following ions.

1. Na^+, Cl^- $NaCl$
2. Ba^{+2}, F^- BaF_2
3. K^+, S^{-2} K_2S
4. Li^+, Br^- $LiBr$
5. Al^{+3}, I^- AlI_3
6. Zn^{+2}, S^{-2} ZnS
7. Ag^+, O^{-2} Ag_2O
8. Mg^{+2}, P^{-3} Mg_3P_2
9. Ni^{+2}, O^{-2} NiO
10. Ni^{+3}, O^{-2} Ni_2O_3
11. Fe^{+2}, O^{-2} FeO
12. Fe^{+3}, O^{-2} Fe_2O_3
13. Cr^{+2}, S^{-2} CrS
14. Cr^{+3}, S^{-2} Cr_2S_3
15. Cu^+, Cl^- $CuCl$
16. Cu^{+2}, Cl^- $CuCl_2$
17. Pb^{+2}, O^{-2} PbO
18. Pb^{+4}, O^{-2} PbO_2
19. Mn^{+2}, Br^- $MnBr_2$
20. Mn^{+4}, Br^- $MnBr_4$

Page 54

NAMING BINARY COMPOUNDS (IONIC)

Name _____

Name the following ionic compounds using Roman numerals where necessary.

1. $BaCl_2$ barium chloride
2. NaF   sodium fluoride
3. Ag_2O silver oxide
4. CuBr   copper (I) bromide
5. $CuBr_2$ copper (II) bromide
6. FeO   iron (II) oxide
7. Fe_2O_3 iron (III) oxide
8. MgS   magnesium sulfide
9. Al_2O_3 aluminum oxide
10. CaI_2 calcium iodide
11. K_2S potassium sulfide
12. $CrCl_2$ chromium (II) chloride
13. $CrCl_3$ chromium (III) chloride
14. CaO   calcium oxide
15. Ba_3P_2 barium phosphide
16. Hg_2I_2 mercury (I) iodide
17. Na_2O sodium oxide
18. BeS   beryllium sulfide
19. MnO   manganese (II) oxide
20. Mn_2O_3 manganese (III) oxide

Page 55

NAMING BINARY COMPOUNDS (COVALENT)

Name _____

Name the following compounds using the prefix method.

1. CO   carbon monoxide
2. CO_2 carbon dioxide
3. SO_2 sulfur dioxide
4. NO_2 nitrogen dioxide
5. N_2O dinitrogen monoxide
6. SO_3 sulfur trioxide
7. CCl_4 carbon tetrachloride
8. NO   nitrogen monoxide
9. N_2O_5 dinitrogen pentoxide
10. P_2O_5 diphosphorus pentoxide
11. N_2O_4 dinitrogen tetroxide
12. CS_2 carbon disulfide
13. OF_2 oxygen difluoride
14. PCl_3 phosphorus trichloride
15. PBr_5 phosphorus pentabromide

Page 56

ANSWER KEY

FORMULAS WITH POLYATOMIC IONS

Name _____

Matching the horizontal and vertical axes, write the formulas of the compounds with the following combination of ions. The first one is done for you.

	OH^-	NO_3^-	CO_3^{-2}	SO_4^{-2}	PO_4^{-3}
H^+	HOH (H_2O)	HNO_3	H_2CO_3	H_2SO_4	H_3PO_4
Na^+	NaOH	$NaNO_3$	Na_2CO_3	Na_2SO_4	Na_3PO_4
Mg^{+2}	$Mg(OH)_2$	$Mg(NO_3)_2$	$MgCO_3$	$MgSO_4$	$Mg_3(PO_4)_2$
NH_4^+	NH_4OH	NH_4NO_3	$(NH_4)_2CO_3$	$(NH_4)_2SO_4$	$(NH_4)_3PO_4$
Ca^{+2}	$Ca(OH)_2$	$Ca(NO_3)_2$	$CaCO_3$	$CaSO_4$	$Ca_3(PO_4)_2$
K^+	KOH	KNO_3	K_2CO_3	K_2SO_4	K_3PO_4
Al^{+3}	$Al(OH)_3$	$Al(NO_3)_3$	$Al_2(CO_3)_3$	$Al_2(SO_4)_3$	$AlPO_4$
Pb^{+2}	$Pb(OH)_4$	$Pb(NO_3)_4$	$Pb(CO_3)_2$	$Pb(SO_4)_2$	$Pb_3(PO_4)_4$

Page 57

NAMING OF NON-BINARY COMPOUNDS

Name _____

An ionic compound that contains more than two elements must contain a polyatomic ion. Name the following compounds.

1. $NaNO_3$ — sodium nitrate
2. $Ca(OH)_2$ — calcium hydroxide
3. K_2CO_3 — potassium carbonate
4. NH_4Cl — ammonium chloride
5. $MgSO_4$ — magnesium sulfate
6. $AlPO_4$ — aluminum phosphate
7. $(NH_4)_2SO_4$ — ammonium sulfate
8. Na_3PO_4 — sodium phosphate
9. $CuSO_4$ — copper (II) sulfate
10. NH_4OH — ammonium hydroxide
11. Li_2SO_3 — lithium sulfite
12. $Mg(NO_3)_2$ — magnesium nitrate
13. $Al(OH)_3$ — aluminum hydroxide
14. $(NH_4)_3PO_4$ — ammonium phosphate
15. KOH — potassium hydroxide
16. $Ca(NO_3)_2$ — calcium nitrate
17. K_2SO_4 — potassium sulfate
18. $Pb(OH)_2$ — lead (II) hydroxide
19. H_2O_2 — sodium peroxide
20. $CuCO_3$ — copper (II) carbonate

Page 58

NAMING COMPOUNDS (MIXED)

Name _____

Name the following compounds.

1. NaCl — Sodium chloride
2. MnS — manganese sulfide
3. K_2O — potassium oxide
4. $CuBr_2$ — Copper (II) bromide
5. CuBr — Copper (I) bromide
6. CO_2 — Carbon dioxide
7. $PbSO_4$ — lead (II) sulfate
8. $LiCO_3$ — lithium carbonate
9. Na_2CO_3 — Sodium carbonate
10. NO_2 — nitrogen dioxide
11. N_2O_4 — dinitrogen tetroxide
12. $Ca(OH)_2$ — Calcium hydroxide
13. NH_4Cl — ammonium chloride
14. SO_3 — sulfur trioxide
15. $AlPO_4$ — aluminum phosphate
16. CCl_4 — Carbon tetrachloride
17. CaS — Calcium sulfide
18. NH_3 — ammonia
19. MgI_2 — magnesium iodide
20. K_3PO_4 — potassium phosphate

Page 59

WRITING FORMULAS FROM NAMES

Name _____

Write the formulas for the following compounds.

1. carbon monoxide — CO
2. sodium chloride — NaCl
3. carbon tetrachloride — CCl_4
4. magnesium bromide — $MgBr_2$
5. aluminum iodide — AlI_3
6. hydrogen hydroxide — HOH
7. iron (II) fluoride — FeF_2
8. carbon dioxide — CO_2
9. sodium carbonate — Na_2CO_3
10. ammonium sulfide — $(NH_4)_2S$
11. iron (II) oxide — FeO
12. iron (III) oxide — Fe_2O_3
13. magnesium sulfate — $MgSO_4$
14. sodium phosphate — Na_3PO_4
15. dinitrogen pentoxide — N_2O_5
16. phosphorus trichloride — PCl_3
17. aluminum sulfite — $Al_2(SO_3)_3$
18. copper (I) carbonate — Cu_2CO_3
19. potassium hydrogen carbonate — $KHCO_3$
20. sulfur trioxide — SO_3

Page 60

ANSWER KEY

BALANCING EQUATIONS

Name _____

Balance the following chemical equations.

1. $CH_4 + 2O_2 \rightarrow CO_2 + 2H_2O$

2. $2Na + I_2 \rightarrow 2NaI$

3. $2N_2 + O_2 \rightarrow 2N_2O$

4. $N_2 + 3H_2 \rightarrow 2NH_3$

5. $2KI + Cl_2 \rightarrow 2KCl + I_2$

6. $2HCl + Ca(OH)_2 \rightarrow CaCl_2 + 2H_2O$

7. $2KClO_3 \rightarrow 2KCl + 3O_2$

8. $K_3PO_4 + 3HCl \rightarrow 3KCl + H_3PO_4$

9. $2S + 3O_2 \rightarrow 2SO_3$

10. $2KI + Pb(NO_3)_2 \rightarrow 2KNO_3 + PbI_2$

11. $3CaSO_4 + 2AlBr_3 \rightarrow 3CaBr_2 + Al_2(SO_4)_3$

12. $2H_2O_2 \rightarrow 2H_2O + O_2$

13. $2Na + 2H_2O \rightarrow 2NaOH + H_2$

14. $2C_2H_6 + 7O_2 \rightarrow 4CO_2 + 6H_2O$

15. $3Mg(NO_3)_2 + 2K_3PO_4 \rightarrow Mg_3(PO_4)_2 + 6KNO_3$

Page 61

WORD EQUATIONS

Name _____

Write and balance the following chemical equations.

1. Hydrogen plus oxygen yields water. $2H_2 + O_2 \rightarrow 2H_2O$

2. Nitrogen plus hydrogen yields ammonia. $N_2 + 3H_2 \rightarrow 2NH_3$

3. Aluminum bromide plus chlorine yields aluminum chloride and bromine. $2AlBr_3 + 3Cl_2 \rightarrow 2AlCl_3 + 3Br_2$

4. Hydrochloric acid plus sodium hydroxide yields sodium chloride plus water. $HCl + NaOH \rightarrow NaCl + H_2O$

5. Iron plus lead (II) sulfate react forming iron (II) sulfate plus lead. $Fe + PbSO_4 \rightarrow FeSO_4 + Pb$

6. Potassium chlorate when heated produces potassium chloride plus oxygen gas. $2KClO_3 \rightarrow 2KCl + 3O_2$

7. Sulfuric acid decomposes to form sulfur trioxide gas plus water. $H_2SO_4 \rightarrow SO_3 + H_2O$

8. Sodium oxide combines with water to make sodium hydroxide. $Na_2O + H_2O \rightarrow 2NaOH$

9. Potassium iodide reacts with bromine forming potassium bromide plus iodine. $2KI + Br_2 \rightarrow 2KBr + I_2$

10. Sodium phosphate reacts with calcium nitrate to produce sodium nitrate plus calcium phosphate. $2Na_3PO_4 + 3Ca(NO_3)_2 \rightarrow 6NaNO_3 + Ca_3(PO_4)_2$

11. Zinc reacts with iron (III) chloride yielding zinc chloride plus iron precipitate. $3Zn + 2FeCl_3 \rightarrow 3ZnCl_2 + 2Fe$

12. Ammonium carbonate and magnesium sulfate react to yield ammonium sulfate plus magnesium carbonate. $(NH_4)_2CO_3 + MgSO_4 \rightarrow (NH_4)_2SO_4 + MgCO_3$

13. Phosphoric acid plus calcium hydroxide react forming solid calcium phosphate plus water. $2H_3PO_4 + 3Ca(OH)_2 \rightarrow Ca_3(PO_4)_2 + 6H_2O$

14. Aluminum plus oxygen gas form aluminum oxide under certain conditions. $4Al + 3O_2 \rightarrow 2Al_2O_3$

15. Nitrogen gas plus oxygen gas react and form dinitrogen pentoxide. $2N_2 + 5O_2 \rightarrow 2N_2O_5$

Page 62

CLASSIFYING CHEMICAL REACTIONS

Name _____

Classify the following reactions as synthesis, decomposition, single replacement or double replacement.

1. $2KClO_3 \rightarrow 2KCl + 3O_2$ — decomposition

2. $HCl + NaOH \rightarrow NaCl + H_2O$ — double replacement

3. $Mg + 2HCl \rightarrow MgCl_2 + H_2$ — single replacement

4. $2H_2 + O_2 \rightarrow 2H_2O$ — synthesis

5. $2Al + 3NiBr_2 \rightarrow 2AlBr_3 + 3Ni$ — single replacement

6. $4Al + 3O_2 \rightarrow 2Al_2O_3$ — synthesis

7. $2NaCl \rightarrow 2Na + Cl_2$ — decomposition

8. $CaCl_2 + F_2 \rightarrow CaF_2 + Cl_2$ — single replacement

9. $AgNO_3 + KCl \rightarrow AgCl + KNO_3$ — double replacement

10. $N_2 + 3H_2 \rightarrow 2NH_3$ — synthesis

11. $2H_2O_2 \rightarrow 2H_2O + O_2$ — decomposition

12. $(NH_4)SO_4 + Ba(NO_3)_2 \rightarrow BaSO_4 + 2NH_4NO_3$ — double replacement

13. $MgI_2 + Br_2 \rightarrow MgBr_2 + I_2$ — single replacement

14. $SO_3 + H_2O \rightarrow H_2SO_4$ — synthesis

15. $6KCl + Zn_3(PO_4)_2 \rightarrow 3ZnCl_2 + 2K_3PO_4$ — double replacement

Page 63

CONSERVATION OF MASS

Name _____

In chemical reactions, mass is neither gained nor lost. The total mass of all the reactants equals the total mass of all the products. Atoms are just rearranged into different compounds.

Using this idea, solve the following problems.

1. $2KClO_3 \rightarrow 2KCl + 3O_2$
   If 500 g of $KClO_3$ decomposes and produces 303 g of KCl, how many grams of O_2 are produced?
   197 g

2. $N_2 + 3H_2 \rightarrow 2NH_3$
   How many grams of H_2 are needed to react with 100 g of N_2 to produce 121 g of NH_3?
   21 g

3. $4Fe + 3O_2 \rightarrow 2Fe_2O_3$
   How many grams of oxygen are needed to react with 350 g of iron to produce 500 g of Fe_2O_3?
   150 g

4. $CH_4 + 2O_2 \rightarrow CO_2 + 2H_2O$
   16 g of CH_4 react with 64 g of O_2, producing 44 g of CO_2. How many grams of water are produced?
   36 g

5. $CaCO_3 \rightarrow CaO + CO_2$
   How much CO_2 is produced from the decomposition of 200 g of $CaCO_3$ if 112 mg of CaO are produced?
   88 g

Page 64

ANSWER KEY

MASS RELATIONSHIPS IN EQUATIONS

Name _____

A balanced equation can tell us the mass relationships involved in a chemical reaction.

Example 1: $2KClO_3 \rightarrow 2KCl + 3O_2$
How many grams of KCl are produced if 244 g of $KClO_3$ decompose?

Solution: 1 formula mass of $KClO_3$ = 122 g
1 formula mass of KCl = 74 g

$$244 \text{ g } KClO_3 \times \frac{2(74 \text{ g}) \text{ KCl}}{2(122 \text{ g}) \text{ } KClO_3} = 148 \text{ g KCl}$$

coefficients from equation

Example 2: $N_2 + 3H_2 \rightarrow 2NH_3$
How many grams of H_2 are needed to react with 56 g of N_2?

Solution: 1 formula mass of N_2 = 28 g
1 formula mass of H_2 = 2 g

$$56 \text{ g } N_2 \times \frac{3(2 \text{ g}) \text{ } H_2}{1(28 \text{ g}) N_2} = 12 \text{ g}$$

Solve the following problems.

1. $2H_2O_2 \rightarrow 2H_2O + O_2$
How many grams of water are produced from the decomposition of 68 g of H_2O_2?

   36 g

2. How many grams of oxygen are produced in the above reaction?

   32 g

3. $2C_2H_6 + 7O_2 \rightarrow 4CO_2 + 6H_2O$
How many grams of oxygen are required to completely react with 120 g of C_2H_6?

   448 g

4. How many grams of CO_2 are produced in the above reaction?

   352 g

5. $2K_3PO_4 + 3MgCl_2 \rightarrow Mg_3(PO_4)_2 + 6KCl$
How much $MgCl_2$ is required to react exactly with 500 g of K_3PO_4?

   333 g

6. How much KCl will be produced in the above reaction?

   524 g

Page 65

ACID, BASE OR SALT

Name _____

Classify each of the following compounds as an acid, base or salt. Then, indicate whether each acid and base is strong or weak.

1.	NHO_3	acid	strong
2.	NaOH	base	strong
3.	$NaNO_3$	salt	
4.	HCl	acid	strong
5.	KCl	salt	
6.	$Ba(OH)_2$	base	strong
7.	KOH	base	strong
8.	H_2S	acid	weak
9.	$Al(NO_3)_3$	salt	
10.	H_2SO_4	acid	strong
11.	$CaCl_2$	salt	
12.	H_3PO_4	acid	weak
13.	Na_2SO_4	salt	
14.	$Mg(OH)_2$	base	strong
15.	H_2CO_3	acid	weak
16.	NH_4OH	base	weak
17.	NH_4Cl	salt	
18.	HBr	acid	strong
19.	$FeBr_3$	salt	
20.	HF	acid	weak

Page 66

pH

Name _____

pH is a scale that measures the hydronium ion concentration of a solution. Therefore, the pH scale can be used to determine the acidity of a solution. A pH of less than 7 indicates an acidic solution, a pH of 7 is neutral, and a pH of greater than 7 up to 14 is basic. The lower the pH, the stronger the acid. The higher the pH, the stronger the base.

Indicators are substances that change color at a different pH levels. Phenolphthalein is colorless in an acid and a neutral solution, pink in a base. Blue litmus changes to red in an acid, and remains blue in neutral and basic solutions. Red litmus remains red in acidic and neutral substances, but turns blue in bases.

Complete the following chart.

pH	Acid, Base, Neutral	Phenolphthalein	Blue Litmus	Red Litmus
2	acid	colorless	red	red
8	base	pink	blue	blue
4	acid	colorless	red	red
7	neutral	colorless	blue	red
13	base	pink	blue	blue
11	base	pink	blue	blue
5	acid	colorless	red	red
1	acid	colorless	red	red

Page 67

pH OF SALT SOLUTIONS

Name _____

A salt is formed from the reaction of an acid and a base.

A strong acid + a strong base $\rightarrow$ neutral salt
A strong acid + a weak base $\rightarrow$ acidic salt
A weak acid + a strong base $\rightarrow$ basic slat

The salt of a weak acid and a weak base may be acidic, neutral or basic, depending on the relative strengths of the acids and bases involved.

The strong acids are HI, HBr, HCl, HNO_3, H_2SO_4 and $HClO_4$. The strong bases are the Group I and Group II hydroxides. All others are considered weak.

Complete the following chart. The first one is done for you.

Salt	Parent Acid	Acid Strength	Parent Base	Base Strength	Type of Salt
KBr	HBr	Strong	KOH	Strong	Neutral
$Fe(NO_3)_2$	HNO_3	Strong	$Fe(OH)_2$	weak	acidic
NaF	HF	weak	NaOH	strong	basic
NH_4Cl	HCl	Strong	NH_4OH	weak	acidic
$Ca(NO_3)_2$	HNO_3	Strong	$Ca(OH)_2$	strong	neutral
Li_3PO_4	H_3PO_4	weak	LiOH	strong	basic
K_2SO_4	H_2SO_4	Strong	KOH	strong	neutral
AlI_3	HI	strong	$Al(OH)_3$	weak	acidic
$MgCO_3$	H_2CO_3	weak	$Mg(OH)_2$	strong	basic
$ZnClO_4$	$HClO_4$	Strong	$Zn(OH)_2$	weak	acidic

Page 68

ANSWER KEY

CONDUCTORS AND ELECTROLYTES

Name _____

Pure metals are good conductors of electricity. Electrolytes are aqueous solutions that conduct electricity. Acids, bases and salts (ionic compounds) are electrolytes. Nonelectrolytes are aqueous solutions that do not conduct electricity. The solutes used to form nonelectrolytes are covalently bonded.

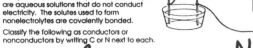

Classify the following as conductors or nonconductors by writing C or N next to each.

1. copper — **C**
2. hydrogen — **N**
3. NaOH(aq) — **C**
4. NaCl(s) — **N**
5. NaCl(aq) — **C**
6. magnesium — **C**
7. H_2SO_4 — **C**
8. NH_4OH — **C**
9. HCl(aq) — **C**
10. $Ca(OH)_2$(aq) — **C**

11. $C_6H_{12}O_6$(aq) — **N**
12. CH_3OH — **N**
13. KNO_3(s) — **N**
14. KNO_3(aq) — **C**
15. chlorine — **N**
16. HNO_3 — **C**
17. $NaNO_3$(aq) — **C**
18. $C_{12}H_{22}O_{11}$ — **N**
19. C_2H_5OH — **N**
20. gold — **C**

EFFECT OF DISSOLVED PARTICLES ON FREEZING AND BOILING POINTS

Name _____

The graph below shows a time/temperature graph for the heating of water. Directly on the graph, sketch the approximate curve that would result when
a) 5 g of sugar ($C_6H_{12}O_6$) are dissolved in the sample;
b) 5 g of NaCl are dissolved;
c) 10g of NaCl are dissolved.

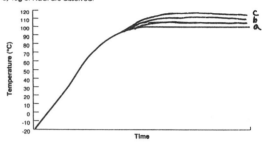

Do the same on the graph below for solutions a, b and c when the solution is cooled through its freezing point.

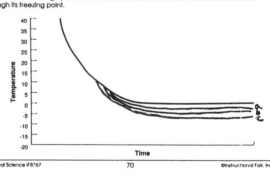

Physical Science IF8767   70   ©Instructional Fair, Inc.

CONCENTRATION (MASS/VOLUME)

Name _____

$$\text{Concentration} = \frac{\text{mass of solute}}{\text{volume of solution}}$$

Solve the following problems.

1. A sugar solution contains 26 g of sugar in 0.50 L of solution. What is the concentration in g/L?

   52 g/L

2. 45 grams of salt are dissolved in 0.10 L of solution. What is the concentration in g/L?

   450 g/L

3. A solution contains 25 g of sugar per liter of solution. How many grams of sugar are in 1.5 L of solution?

   37.5 g

4. A solution contains 85 g of corn syrup per liter of solution. How many grams of corn syrup are in 500 mL of solution?

   42.5 g

5. How many liters of salt solution would be needed to provide 30 g of salt if the concentration of the solution is 20 g/L?

   1.5 L

CONCENTRATION (% BY VOLUME)

Name _____

$$\% \text{ volume} = \frac{V_{solute}}{V_{total}} \times 100\%$$

Solve the following problems. Assume all volumes are additive.

1. 25 mL of ethanol is added to enough water to make 100 mL of solution. Find the percent by volume of ethanol.

   25 %

2. 50 mL of ethanol is added to 50 mL of water. What is the percent by volume of ethanol?

   50 %

3. 3.0 liters of antifreeze is added to 4.0 liters of water. Find the percent by volume of antifreeze.

   43 %

4. A popular fruit drink contains 5% by volume fruit juice. How much fruit juice is in 500 mL of the fruit drink?

   25 mL

5. How much corn syrup should be added to water to make 200 mL of a 10% by volume solution?

   20 mL

ANSWER KEY

CONCENTRATION (% BY MASS)

Name _____

$$\text{Concentration} = \frac{\text{mass of solute}}{\text{Mass of solution}} \times 100\%$$

Solve the following problems.

1. 25 g of sugar in 75 g of solution will have what percent by mass of sugar?

   33%

2. 35 g of salt is dissolved in 500 g of total solution. What is the percent by mass of salt?

   7%

3. 50 g of sugar are dissolved in 50 g of water. What is the percent by mass of sugar?

   50%

4. 75 g of potassium nitrate are dissolved in 150 g of water. What is the percent by mass of potassium nitrate?

   33%

5. How many grams of sodium bromide are in 200 g of a solution that is 15% sodium bromide by mass?

   30 g

Page 73

SOLUBILITY

Name _____

Classify the following compounds as soluble or insoluble following the rules for solubility.

1. $AgNO_3$ — **soluble**
2. K_2CO_3 — **soluble**
3. $Ca_3(PO_4)_2$ — **insoluble**
4. $AgCl$ — **insoluble**
5. $NaOH$ — **soluble**
6. NH_4Cl — **soluble**
7. KBr — **soluble**
8. $MgCO_3$ — **insoluble**
9. FeS — **insoluble**
10. $CuC_2H_3O_2$ — **soluble**
11. $(NH_4)_2SO_4$ — **soluble**
12. $Ca(OH)_2$ — **insoluble**
13. Na_2SO_4 — **soluble**
14. $BaSO_4$ — **insoluble**
15. KI — **soluble**
16. $(NH_4)_3PO_4$ — **soluble**
17. $Cu(NO_3)_2$ — **soluble**
18. $AlPO_4$ — **insoluble**
19. $CaCO_3$ — **insoluble**
20. $(NH_4)_2S$ — **soluble**

Page 74

NAMING ORGANIC COMPOUNDS

Name _____

Name the following organic compounds.

1. **methane**
2. **propene**
3. **ethyne**
4. **ethane**
5. **1-butene**
6. **propane**
7. **propyne**
8. **ethene**

Page 75

DRAWING STRUCTURAL FORMULAS

Name _____

Draw the structural formula of the following compounds.

1. ethane
2. propene
3. 1-butyne
4. ethene
5. propyne
6. methane
7. ethyne
8. 1-pentene

Page 76

ANSWER KEY

ISOMERS   Name _____

Isomers have the same chemical formula but different structural formulas. Match the structure in Column I with its isomer in Column II.

I   **II**

1.
```
    H   H   H
    |   |   |
H — C — C — C — OH
    |   |   |
    H   H   H
```
b

a)
```
    H  CH₃  H
    |   |   |
H — C — C — C — H
    |   |   |
    H   H   H
```

2.
```
    H   O   H
    |   ‖   |
H — C — C — C — H
    |       |
    H       H
```
d

b)
```
    H  OH  H
    |   |   |
H — C — C — C — H
    |   |   |
    H   H   H
```

3.
```
    H   H   H   H
    |   |   |   |
H — C — C — C — C — H
    |   |   |   |
    H   H   H   H
```
a

c)
```
      CH₃
       |
H₃C — C — CH₃
       |
      CH₃
```

4.
```
    H   H   H   H   H
    |   |   |   |   |
H — C — C — C — C — C — H
    |   |   |   |   |
    H   H   H   H   H
```
c

d)
```
    H   H   O
    |   |   ‖
H — C — C — C — H
    |   |
    H   H
```

5.
```
    H   O
    |   ‖
H — C — C — OH
    |
    H
```
e

e)
```
    H       O
    |       ‖
H — C — O — C — H
    |
    H
```

Page 77

ORGANIC CHEMISTRY CROSSWORD   Name _____

Across
4. Compound containing only carbon and hydrogen
6. Produced when one or more of the hydrogens in a hydrocarbon is replaced by a hydroxide
7. All carbon atoms are joined by single covalent bonds
8. Sugar and starch
9. Long chains of carbon atoms produced by joining small chains together
10. Ingredient of gasoline

Down
1. Compounds with the same chemical formula but different structures
2. Organic compounds in the body used to store energy
3. Compound containing a double or triple covalent bond
5. Polymer made from smaller molecules called amino acids
9. Mixture of hydrocarbons that are used for fuels

Page 78

WAVE DIAGRAM   Name _____

On the following diagram, place the following terms in their correct places: amplitude, wavelength, crest, trough, rest position.

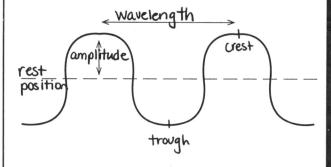

Define the terms below.

amplitude—the distance a wave rises or falls from its rest position

wavelength—the distance from a point on one wave to the corresponding point on the next wave

crest—the highest point on a wave

trough—the lowest point on a wave

Page 79

WAVE VELOCITY CALCULATIONS   Name _____

Velocity = Wavelength x Frequency

Solve the following problems

1. A tuning fork has a frequency of 280 hertz, and the wavelength of the sound produced is 1.5 meters. Calculate the velocity of the wave.

   420 m/s

2. A wave is moving toward shore with a velocity of 5.0 m/s. If its frequency is 2.5 hertz, what is its wavelength?

   2.0 m

3. The speed of light is 3.0×10^8 m/s. Red light has a wavelength of 7×10^{-7} m. What is its frequency?

   4.3×10^{14} hertz

4. The frequency of violet light is 7.5×10^{14} hertz. What is its wavelength?

   4×10^{-7} m

5. A jump rope is shaken producing a wave with a wavelength of 0.5 m with the crest of the wave passing a certain point 4 times per second. What is the velocity of the wave?

   2 m/s

Page 80

ANSWER KEY

SOUND AND MUSIC CROSSWORD

Name _____

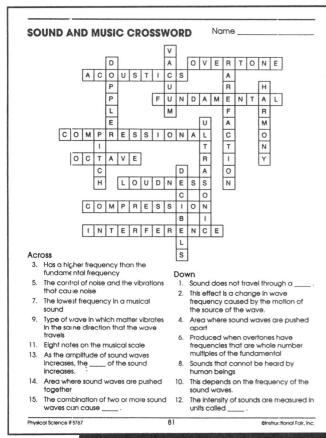

Across
3. Has a higher frequency than the fundamental frequency
5. The control of noise and the vibrations that cause noise
7. The lowest frequency in a musical sound
9. Type of wave in which matter vibrates in the same direction that the wave travels
11. Eight notes on the musical scale
13. As the amplitude of sound waves increases, the ____ of the sound increases.
14. Area where sound waves are pushed together
15. The combination of two or more sound waves can cause ____ .

Down
1. Sound does not travel through a ____ .
2. This effect is a change in wave frequency caused by the motion of the source of the wave.
4. Area where sound waves are pushed apart
6. Produced when overtones have frequencies that are whole number multiples of the fundamental
8. Sounds that cannot be heard by human beings
10. This depends on the frequency of the sound waves.
12. The intensity of sounds are measured in units called ____ .

Page 81

REFLECTION

Name _____

Draw the expected path of the light rays as they reflect off the following plane mirrors.

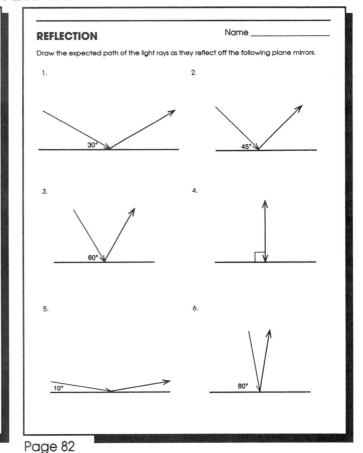

Page 82

REFRACTION

Name _____

Draw the pathway of the light beam as it passes through each of the following substances. Using a protractor, measure the refracted angle.

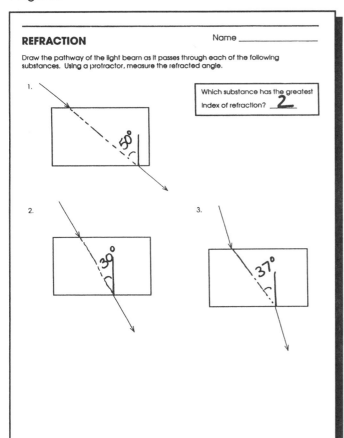

Which substance has the greatest index of refraction? **2**

Page 83

LIGHT RAYS AND CONVEX LENSES

Name _____

Draw the pathways of the light from the objects on the left through the convex lenses. Label the focal point and the inverted image.

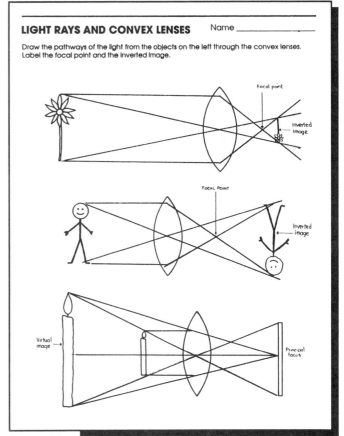

Page 84

ANSWER KEY

LIGHT RAYS AND CONCAVE LENSES   Name _____

Draw the path of light through the concave lenses below. Label the image and focal point.

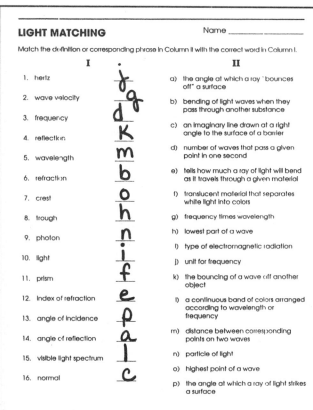

WHITE LIGHT SPECTRUM   Name _____

Label the colors coming through this prism as the white light is reflected through it.

a) **red**
b) **orange**
c) **yellow**
d) **green**
e) **blue**
f) **Indigo**
g) **violet**

LIGHT MATCHING   Name _____

Match the definition or corresponding phrase in Column II with the correct word in Column I.

I		II
1. hertz	j	a) the angle at which a ray "bounces off" a surface
2. wave velocity	g	b) bending of light waves when they pass through another substance
3. frequency	d	c) an imaginary line drawn at a right angle to the surface of a barrier
4. reflection	k	d) number of waves that pass a given point in one second
5. wavelength	m	e) tells how much a ray of light will bend as it travels through a given material
6. refraction	b	f) translucent material that separates white light into colors
7. crest	o	g) frequency times wavelength
8. trough	h	h) lowest part of a wave
9. photon	n	i) type of electromagnetic radiation
10. light	i	j) unit for frequency
11. prism	f	k) the bouncing of a wave off another object
12. index of refraction	e	l) a continuous band of colors arranged according to wavelength or frequency
13. angle of incidence	p	m) distance between corresponding points on two waves
14. angle of reflection	a	n) particle of light
15. visible light spectrum	l	o) highest point of a wave
16. normal	c	p) the angle at which a ray of light strikes a surface

MAGNETIC FIELDS   Name _____

Draw the pattern of magnetic fields around these magnets

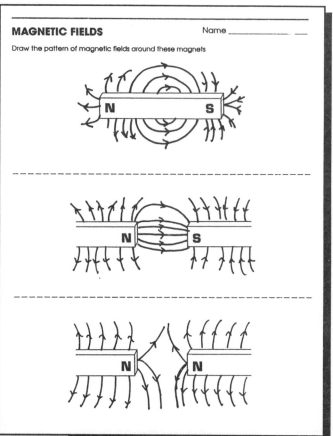

ANSWER KEY

CALCULATING CURRENT

Name _____

Ohm's Law states that $I = \dfrac{V}{R}$

where I = current (amperes)
V = voltage (volts)
R = resistance (ohms)

Solve the following problems.

1. What is the current produced with a 9-volt battery through a resistance of 100 ohms?

0.09 amps

2. Find the current when a 12-volt battery is connected through a resistance of 25 ohms.

0.48 amps

3. If the potential difference is 120 volts and the resistance is 50 ohms, what is the current?

2.4 amps

4. What would be the current in Problem 3 if the potential difference were doubled?

4.8 amps

5. What would be the current in Problem 3 if the resistance were doubled?

1.2 amps

Page 89

CALCULATING VOLTAGE

Name _____

V = I x R
Voltage (volts) = Current (amperes) x Resistance (ohms)

Solve the following problems.

1. What voltage produces a current of 50 amps with a resistance of 20 ohms?

1,000 volts

2. Silver has a resistance of 1.98×10^{-4} ohms. What voltage would produce a current of 100 amps?

0.0198 volts

3. A current of 250 amps is flowing through a copper wire with a resistance of 2.09×10^{-4} ohms. What is the voltage?

0.0523 volts

4. What voltage produces a current of 500 maps with a resistance of 50 ohms?

25,000 volts

5. What voltage would produce a current of 100 amps through an aluminum wire which has a resistance of 3.44×10^{-4} ohms?

0.0344 volts

Page 90

CALCULATING RESISTANCE

Name _____

$R = \dfrac{V}{I}$ Resistance (ohms) = $\dfrac{\text{Voltage (volts)}}{\text{Current (amperes)}}$

Solve the following problems.

1. What resistance would produce a current of 200 amperes with a potential difference of 2,000 volts?

10 ohms

2. A 12-volt battery produces a current of 25 amperes. What is the resistance?

0.48 ohms

3. A 9-volt battery produces a current of 2.0 amperes. What is the resistance?

4.5 ohms

4. An overhead wire has a potential difference of 2,000 volts. If the current flowing through the wire is one million amperes, what is the resistance of the wire?

0.002 ohms

5. What is the resistance of a light bulb if a 120-volt potential difference produces a current of 0.8 amperes?

150 ohms

Page 91

OHM'S LAW PROBLEMS

Name _____

Using Ohm's Law, solve the following problems.

1. What is the current produced by a potential difference of 240 volts through a resistance of 0.2 ohms?

1,200 amperes

2. What resistance would produce a current of 120 amps from a 6-volt battery?

0.05 ohms

3. What voltage is necessary to produce a current of 200 amperes through a resistance of 1×10^{-3} ohms?

0.2 volts

4. What is the current produced by a 9-volt battery flowing through a resistance of 2×10^{-4} ohms?

45,000 amps

5. What is the potential difference if a resistance of 25 ohms produces a current of 250 amperes?

6,250 volts

Page 92

ANSWER KEY

CALCULATING POWER

Name _____

$$P = V \times I$$
Power (watts) = Voltage (voltage) x current (amperes)

Solve the following problems.

1. A 6-volt battery produces a current of 0.5 amps. What is the power in the circuit?

   3 watts

2. A 100-watt light bulb is operating on 1.2 amperes current. What is the voltage?

   83 volts

3. A potential difference of 120 volts is operating on a 500-watt microwave oven. What is the current being used?

   4.2 amps

4. A light bulb uses 0.625 amperes from a source of 120 volts. How much power is used by the bulb?

   75 watts

5. What voltage is necessary to run a 500-watt motor with a current of 200 amperes?

   2.5 volts

CALCULATING ELECTRICAL ENERGY AND COST

Name _____

One kilowatt hour is 1,000 watts of power for one hour of time. The abbreviation for kilowatt hour is kWh.

> **Example:** A coffee pot operates on 2 amperes of current on a 110-volt circuit for 3 hours. Calculate the total kWh used.
> 1. Determine power: P = V x I   kWh = P x hours
>   = 110 volts x 2 amps   kWh = $\dfrac{V \times I \times hours}{1,000}$
>   = 220 watts
> 2. Convert watts to kilowatts:
>   220 watts x $\dfrac{1\ kilowatt}{1,000\ watts}$ = 0.22 kW
> 3. Multiply by the hours given in the problem:
>   0.22 kW x 3 hrs = 0.66 kWh

Solve the following problems.

1. A microwave oven operates on 5 amps of current on a 110-volt circuit for one hour. Calculate the total kilowatt hours used. _____ **0.55 kWh**

2. How much would it cost to run the microwave in Problem 1 if the cost of energy is $0.10 per kWh? **$0.06**

3. An electric stove operates on 20 amps of current on a 220-volt circuit for one hour. Calculate the total kilowatt hours used. **4.4 kWh**

4. What is the cost of using the stove in Problem 3 if the cost of energy if $0.10 per kWh? _____ **$0.44**

5. A refrigerator operates on 15 amps of current on a 220 volt circuit for 18 hours per day. How many kilowatt hours are used per day? _____ **59.4 kWh**

6. If the electric costs are 15¢ per kWh, how much does it cut to run the refrigerator in Problem 5 per day? _____ **$8.91**

7. The meter reading on June 1 was 84502 kWh. On July 1, the meter read 87498 kWh. If the cost of electricity in the area was 12¢ per kWh, what was the electric bill for the month of June? **$359.52**

8. A room was lifted with three 100-watt bulbs for 5 hours per day. If the cost of electricity was 9¢ per kWh, how much would be saved per day by switching to 60-watt bulbs? **$0.05   (5.5¢)**

SERIES AND PARALLEL CIRCUITS

Name _____

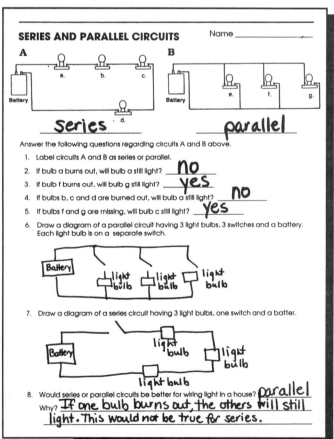

series   **parallel**

Answer the following questions regarding circuits A and B above.

1. Label circuits A and B as series or parallel.
2. If bulb a burns out, will bulb a still light? **no**
3. If bulb f burns out, will bulb g still light? **yes**
4. If bulbs b, c and d are burned out, will bulb a still light? **no**
5. If bulbs f and g are missing, will bulb c still light? **yes**
6. Draw a diagram of a parallel circuit having 3 light bulbs, 3 switches and a battery. Each light bulb is on a separate switch.

7. Draw a diagram of a series circuit having 3 light bulbs, one switch and a batter.

8. Would series or parallel circuits be better for wiring light in a house? **parallel**
   Why? **If one bulb burns out, the others will still light. This would not be true for series.**

AN ELECTRIC MOTOR

Name _____

Label the following parts on the picture of the electric motor below. List the function/purpose of each part.

horseshoe electromagnet (or permanent magnet)—produces a magnetic field so wire loop will rotate

armature—many loops of wire wound around an iron cylinder, which rotates as current flows through wire

commutator—switches direction of current flow, so poles of magnet are reversed

brushes (+ and –)—supply current to the commutator

field coil—strengthens electromagnetic field

current source—supplies current to coil, so it becomes a magnet

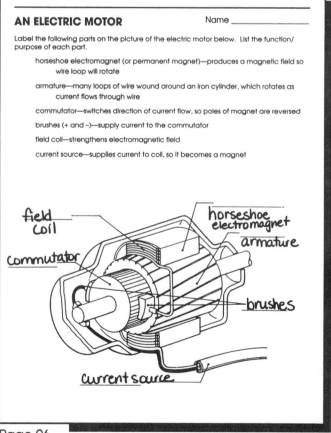

ANSWER KEY

AN ELECTRIC GENERATOR

Name _____

Label the following parts on the picture of the diagrams below of an alternating current and a direct current generator. List the function/purpose of each part.

wire coils—create an electric field which interacts with the magnet

brushes—conduct current from slip rings to wires

slip rings (A.C. only)—conduct current from armature to brushes

commutator (D.C. only)—changes A.C. current to D.C. current

armature—strengthen fields so current will flow

magnet—provides magnetic field through which armature is rotated

Direct Current

wire coils
armature
Commutator
magnet
brushes

Alternating Current

wire coils
armature
slip rings
magnet
brushes

Page 97

TRANSFORMERS

Name _____

Determine the voltage and current in the following transformers.

Step-Up Transformer

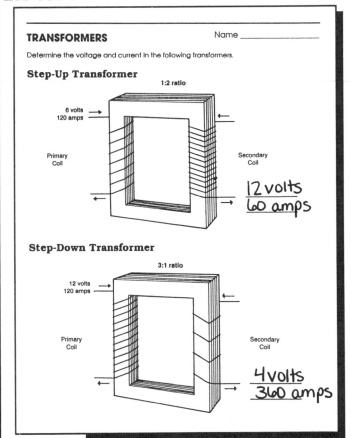

1:2 ratio

6 volts
120 amps

Primary Coil

Secondary Coil

12 volts
60 amps

Step-Down Transformer

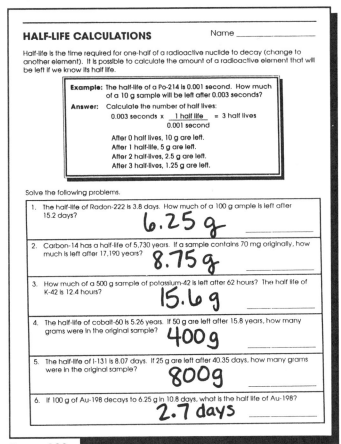

3:1 ratio

12 volts
120 amps

Primary Coil

Secondary Coil

4 volts
360 amps

Page 98

ELECTRICITY CROSSWORD

Name _____

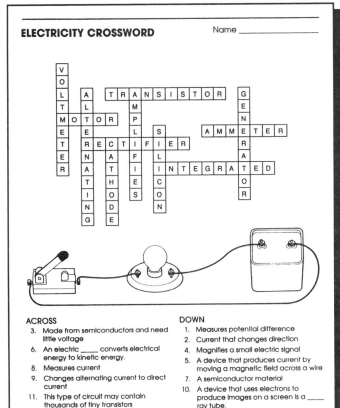

Crossword grid with answers:
VOLTMETER (down)
ALTERNATING (down)
TRANSISTOR (across)
MOTOR (across)
AMPLIFIER
RECTIFIER (across)
AMMETER (across)
SILICON
INTEGRATED (across)
GENERATOR (down)
DIODE

ACROSS

3. Made from semiconductors and need little voltage
6. An electric ____ converts electrical energy to kinetic energy.
8. Measures current
9. Changes alternating current to direct current
11. This type of circuit may contain thousands of tiny transistors

DOWN

1. Measures potential difference
2. Current that changes direction
4. Magnifies a small electric signal
5. A device that produces current by moving a magnetic field across a wire
7. A semiconductor material
10. A device that uses electrons to produce images on a screen is a ____ ray tube.

Page 99

HALF-LIFE CALCULATIONS

Name _____

Half-life is the time required for one-half of a radioactive nuclide to decay (change to another element). It is possible to calculate the amount of a radioactive element that will be left if we know its half life.

> **Example:** The half-life of a Po-214 is 0.001 second. How much of a 10 g sample will be left after 0.003 seconds?
>
> **Answer:** Calculate the number of half lives:
>
> $$0.003 \text{ seconds} \times \frac{1 \text{ half life}}{0.001 \text{ second}} = 3 \text{ half lives}$$
>
> After 0 half lives, 10 g are left.
> After 1 half-life, 5 g are left.
> After 2 half-lives, 2.5 g are left.
> After 3 half-lives, 1.25 g are left.

Solve the following problems.

1. The half-life of Radon-222 is 3.8 days. How much of a 100 g ample is left after 15.2 days?

   6.25 g

2. Carbon-14 has a half-life of 5,730 years. If a sample contains 70 mg originally, how much is left after 17,190 years?

   8.75 g

3. How much of a 500 g sample of potassium-42 is left after 62 hours? The half life of K-42 is 12.4 hours?

   15.6 g

4. The half-life of cobalt-60 is 5.26 years. If 50 g are left after 15.8 years, how many grams were in the original sample?

   400 g

5. The half-life of I-131 is 8.07 days. If 25 g are left after 40.35 days, how many grams were in the original sample?

   800 g

6. If 100 g of Au-198 decays to 6.25 g in 10.8 days, what is the half life of Au-198?

   2.7 days

Page 100

ANSWER KEY

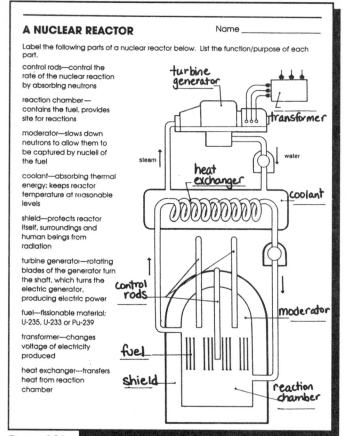

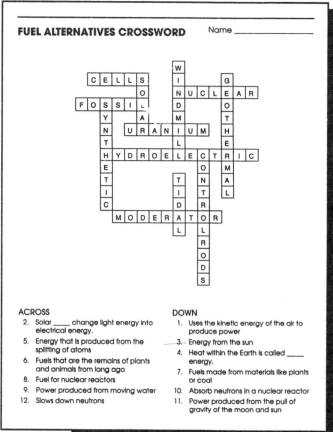

FUEL ALTERNATIVES CROSSWORD

ACROSS

2. Solar _____ change light energy into electrical energy.
5. Energy that is produced from the splitting of atoms
6. Fuels that are the remains of plants and animals from long ago
8. Fuel for nuclear reactors
9. Power produced from moving water
12. Slows down neutrons

DOWN

1. Uses the kinetic energy of the air to produce power
3. Energy from the sun
4. Heat within the Earth is called _____ energy.
7. Fuels made from materials like plants or coal
10. Absorb neutrons in a nuclear reactor
11. Power produced from the pull of gravity of the moon and sun

About the Book ...

A valuable resource for any teacher introducing chemistry and physics to young students. This book contains activities and practice on metrics, graphing, motion, machines, the periodic table, formulas and equations, light, electricity and much more.

About the Author ...

Joan DiStasio has a Master's degree in Chemistry Education and is a high school science teacher. She has also worked for the chemical industry and has edited several professional books in the science field.

Credits ...

Author: Joan DiStasio
Artist: Don O'Connor
Project Director: Mina McMullin
Editors: Kathy Lister, Mary Jo Kohunsky
Graphic Design: Jill Kaufman
Production: Janie Schmidt
Cover Photo: ©Comstock, Inc. 1994
Cover Production: Annette Hollister-Papp